THE EMERGING LAYMAN

The Emerging Layman:

THE ROLE OF THE CATHOLIC LAYMAN IN AMERICA

DONALD J. THORMAN

DOUBLEDAY & COMPANY, INC.

GARDEN CITY, NEW YORK

Nihil obstat: James F. Rigney, S. T. D.
Censor Librorum

Imprimatur:✠ Francis Cardinal Spellman
Archbishop of New York

May 15, 1962

The *nihil obstat* and *imprimatur* are official declarations that a book or pamphlet is free of doctrinal or moral error. No implication is contained therein that those who have granted the *nihil obstat* and *imprimatur* agree with the contents, opinions, or statements expressed.

Excerpt from an editorial appearing on October 30, 1959, in *Commonweal*, reprinted by permission.

Excerpts from an address by John Courtney Murray to the Thomas More Association. Copyright, 1956, the Thomas More Association, reprinted from *The Critic* magazine.

Excerpt from *Protestant Hopes and the Catholic Responsibility* by the Rev. George Tavard. Reprinted with permission of Fides Publishers, Notre Dame, Indiana.

Excerpts from *Free Speech in the Church* by Karl Rahner, S.J., © Sheed & Ward, Inc., 1959, New York and Sheed & Ward, Ltd., London.

DEDICATION

To my mother and father, who made it all possible.

To my wife, Barbara. She was both mother and father to our children during 1961 when this book was being written. In a very real sense this is her book as much as it is mine.

And to our children—Peggy, Judy, Jim, Betsy, Dave, Dan, and Damian. More than once that summer they were asked, "Where are you going or what are you doing for your vacation?" And they answered without complaint, "Oh, we aren't doing anything. Daddy's writing a book." When they are old enough to read and understand these pages I hope they will feel Daddy's efforts and their sacrifices were all worth it.

ACKNOWLEDGMENTS

To attempt to acknowledge all the many persons and influences that have affected me, and thus this book, would be an unending as well as a pointless task. But I would indeed be remiss if I did not mention: Father John M. Hayes, counselor of old and a writer himself, who introduced me to the first editor I ever knew; the Holy Cross Fathers who allowed me to take an active part as managing editor of *Ave Maria* magazine in many of the lay movements and apostolates I mention in this book; Msgr. John J. Egan, friend of the lay apostolate, and a friend in need; the Claretian Fathers, especially as represented by the late Joachim De Prada, C.M.F., who gave me my first real job in the Catholic press as managing editor of *St. Jude* magazine; and in a very special way Dan Herr, president of the Thomas More Association, who coaxed, cajoled, persuaded, encouraged, and advised me until this book was completed. He is a witty and lively foe of platitudes, but it is no platitude to say that without his continuing interest I doubt this book would ever have come into being.

The author also wishes to express his sincere thanks to the editors of *America*, *Spiritual Life*, and *Today*, who were kind enough to grant him permission to use material previously published in these magazines.

CONTENTS

THE EMERGING LAYMAN

CHAPTER 1

The Apostolate of the Laity

The American Catholic layman stands on the threshold of a new and exciting era. Behind him lie centuries of Church history, a record of grace and heroism and sanctity. And ahead is the time God has allotted to the world with the record yet to be written—to be written in no little part by the laymen of the Church in America.

We do not have to be told that these are exciting times, days filled with currents and crosscurrents, pulsating and vibrating with the life of divine grace. It is good to be alive, to be able to serve the Church, our country, and the world in times when some of the most far-reaching history of mankind is being made. And what the history books will contain a century from now depends in no small part on how we act in our lifetime, how we respond to the challenge, how we put into effect in the twentieth century the logical consequences of our beliefs.

Yet, faced with the enormity and the breathtaking scope of the tasks facing us as Christians in the midst of a secular and unchristian world, all of us are inclined to ask: "Why? Why must I do these things which take so much time and effort? Why can't the Church do them?" We are always a little afraid before the prospect of a deep and lifelong personal commitment that requires much of us. So we want to be persuaded, we want to be convinced.

The fact is, however, that we are already committed; we were committed to Christ on the day of our baptism.

Every layman, says Bishop Leo A. Pursley of Fort Wayne-South Bend, Indiana, must "appreciate the full meaning of his membership in the Church, of his incorporation by baptism into the living Body of Christ, a royal and priestly society; of his promotion by Confirmation to the rank and responsibility of a true apostle, an official witness of divine truth, not in the strict sense of the sacramental priesthood, but in the proper sphere of the layman's life, not at the altar of the Church, but in the sanctuary of the home, not from the pulpit, but from every single point of vantage open to the layman in the associations of his private and public life. No less than the ordained priest, the layman has a religious vocation, a mission, a mandate to speak and work for Christ."

Through baptism, when our share in the divine life of the Trinity began to course through our soul, we were marked with the mark of Christ. Through Confirmation—the sacrament of the lay apostolate—the Holy Spirit came, with His divine gifts, to make us full-fledged soldiers of Christ, Christian missionaries to the world. We no longer *belong* to the Church, we *are* the Church.

To the cardinals he created in 1946, Pope Pius XII commented: "The faithful, and more precisely the laity, are stationed in the front ranks of the life of the Church, and through them the Church is the living principle of human society. Consequently, they especially must have an ever clearer consciousness, not only of belonging to the Church, but of being the Church."

Once we actually appreciate this profound truth, we can understand that as baptized, confirmed members of the Church—the Mystical Body of Christ on earth—we are literally Christ-bearers. We cannot remain aloof from the world, uninterested and not caring, any more than Christ could. We can no longer think of ourselves as isolated individuals, for through us the Church—Christ in His Mystical Body on earth—"is the living principle of human society."

In his pioneering book on the lay apostolate, *The Layman's Call*, published some twenty years ago, Father William O'Connor pointed out: "To be a Christian is in itself a vocation, since no one can accept the Gospel of Christ unless he is first called by God." And he added: "This vocation does not stop with baptism. A Christian is called upon to 'put on Christ':

to identify himself with Christ in his life and conduct. He is to live in Christ, and Christ is to live in him. Every baptized person is called upon to live up to all the requirements of the Christian profession, to practice the Christian virtues in season and out of season, and to lead a perfect life no matter what his position or standing in the world may be."

And as laymen we have a further vocation—to bring Christ to the world. In the words of Cardinal Suhard, the late Archbishop of Paris: "The laity have an irreplaceable work to do. They have their own witness to bear, their specific problems to solve and reforms to bring about, for all of which they are solely responsible."

We find ourselves today at a point in history where the role and dignity of the laity are a matter of deep concern for the clergy and the laity alike. Thirty years of dramatic and unprecedented development of the lay apostolate in this country has been accompanied by increasing papal interest. When Pope Pius XII spoke to the First World Congress of the Lay Apostolate in Rome in 1951, anyone who would have predicted what has actually happened between then and now probably would have been regarded as a dreamer. But it is a matter of record that years of growth seem to have been telescoped into a single decade.

In analyzing what has happened it is helpful to make use of a tool that the sociologists have developed in the study of social problems—the "natural history" of a social problem. That is, by studying a wide variety of social situations they have arrived at some common characteristics that distinguish a social problem.

The first of these characteristics is an awareness on the part of a number of persons that a problem exists. People begin to say that something ought to be done about the situation.

Second, a period of debate begins in which there is a great deal of discussion over the determination of a policy to be followed in attempting to find a solution to the problem. This discussion takes place on three levels: Among the people involved and various other unorganized groups; among organized groups which have some interest in the problem; and, finally, among official governmental groups.

The last characteristic is the period of actually meeting the problem on the basis of the policy decided upon in the second stage of the natural history.

If it is possible to apply this thinking to the problem of the layman's role in the Church, it is clear to see that within the past ten years we have jumped from the first well into the second stage. Discussion of this whole question of the role of the laity and the lay apostolate is to the eager young Catholics of today what the social teachings of the Church were to the Catholics looking for answers during the days of the Great Depression. Books, magazine articles, and pamphlets contribute to contemporary thinking on the laity. Study clubs and adult education classes are mulling it over.

And, as we have seen, occasional discussions among the younger set are not all. The papacy speaks on it. Members of the hierarchy are turning their attention to the subject more and more. Pastoral letters are concerned with it. Groups meet to discuss it formally. And national and international congresses of the laity plan meetings to get interested persons to delve its depths. Finally, the announcement by Pope John early in 1961 that the Second Vatican Council would pay special attention to the layman's role indicates that in the not too distant future we should be completing the second stage.

To keep our proper perspective, we must realize, of course, that the contemporary history we are helping shape is building on some ancient history and ideas. The lay apostolate is, after all, not a new idea coined by twentieth century Christians. As Cardinal Richard J. Cushing has noted:

"St. Paul gives us the theology of it: 'For just as in one body we have many members, yet all members have not the same function, so we, the many, are one body in Christ, but severally members one of another. But we have gifts differing according to the grace that has been given us, such as prophecy to be used according to the proportion of the faith; or ministry, in ministering; or he who teaches, in teaching; he who exhorts, in exhorting; he who gives, in simplicity; he who presides, with carefulness; he who shows mercy, with cheerfulness.'"

The lay apostolate was never lost in the history of the Church—either in theory or practice. But it was certainly submerged after the fourth century. At this time the West became a Christian society with Catholic rulers and this resulted in a certain loss of separation between the Church and the temporal order. Then following the Reformation the emphasis was understandably on the official Church as opposed to Protestantism's accent on the layman and individualism.

In its modern history, Miss Rosemary Goldie, executive secretary of the Permanent Committee for International Congresses of the Lay Apostolate in Rome, traces it this way:

The first half of the nineteenth century, which was marked by rapid development of the individual apostolate;

The reign of Pope Pius IX, which was characterized by the rise of Catholic associations for the defense of the Church against enemies from without;

The period from the reign of Pope Leo XIII to the reign of Pope Pius XI, marked by the development of Christian social action and of Catholic Action;

And, finally, the reign of Pope Pius XI, in which Catholic Action was defined as an apostolate in the strict sense. It was marked by the rise of specialized movements.

Commenting on this last phase, Miss Goldie told a lay apostolate meeting in Copenhagen in late 1960: "We are still today in this last period, if not on the threshold of a new stage. Enriched by the teaching of Pope Pius XII and strengthened by the encouragement and directives of Pope John XXIII, it may be that the lay apostolate is about to bring forth in fullness the fruits of this century of growth, and above all of these last forty years, during which the role of the laity in the Church's apostolic mission has been not only deeply studied but also experienced in manifold terms."

So, in a way, the lay apostolate has come full circle. Like our first-century Christian forebears we face a world that is largely without Christ. And also like them we face this world as missionaries of the Risen Christ.

"If there ever was a time in the history of the Church when we needed our laymen to work, to sense their responsibility and to help us in the apostolate of the Church, that time is today," the late Samuel Cardinal Stritch told a group of Chicago laymen in 1955. And he added that the Catholic has no choice in the matter. "The very fact that he's a Catholic layman imposes upon him an obligation to do his full part for the Kingdom of Christ."

Yet, I daresay that despite all the interest and activity among the Catholic laity of the United States there is no term more misunderstood than "lay apostolate." For most of us the lay apostolate remains an interesting but rarefied term—something like the liturgy, intriguing but unrelated to everyday life.

In the minds of many, a lay apostle is still regarded as a kind of frustrated priest, a priest's helper, a hanger-on at the fringes of the clerical ranks. For others, a lay apostle is one who "compensates" for his work in the secular world by giving his worldly talents to the service of the Church on appropriate occasions. For still others, he is someone who is filling in, doing the work that properly belongs to the clergy, helping to hold the fort until there are enough vocations so that he may be relieved and go back to his more proper, passive way of life. All of these are caricatures of reality; unfortunately, however, they are taken for reality itself by many Catholics.

If these conceptions do not describe the lay apostolate, what then is the true role of the laity, the layman's genuine function?

The Catholic layman's real and special role is to mediate between the Church and civil society, to reconcile the two societies, to be the link between them. The laity are full-blown, legitimate members of both societies and short of divine intervention they are the only means by which Christ and Christian principles will be made a part of the temporal order, the society in which we live.

It is the laity's task to make Christ live in the world. They must bring Him into the major social institutions—family life, education, recreation, economic and political affairs; and even within the realm of religious affairs laymen have a special part to play.

The layman must see the world whole and he must see himself in the context of the world and the Church. He has a foot in both camps; he has an allegiance to both. If he is an integrated Christian who attempts to see the world through Christ's eyes, he will see Christ and his eternal destiny on the far-off foothills of heaven. Leading to Christ are two parallel paths which he must tread, one foot in each—the paths of the Church and the temporal order. He is the link connecting these two paths. He has a body and a soul. He must contribute to both aspects of his nature.

His long-range goal is to save his soul. But he does this by attempting to make Christ incarnate in the world during his brief life-span. He achieves his goal through his religion and through his life in the world, according to the talents and abilities God gave him.

"The lay apostolate consists in this," Pope Pius XII told the Second World Congress of the Lay Apostolate in 1957, "that laymen undertake tasks deriving from the mission Christ entrusted to His Church."

What does this mean in concrete terms? A brief look at the lay apostolate as recent Popes seem to visualize it and as it is working out in practice today will help give us the answer.

The most obvious form of the apostolate is that within the Church and under the direct control of the Church, at least to the degree that the very existence of the work or organization is dependent upon the approval of the bishop in whose diocese it exists. (We are speaking here primarily of the organized apostolates and not of the more personal apostolates of prayer and good example, which Pope Pius XII has pointed out as suitable and obligatory for everyone.)

The Legion of Mary, the Confraternity of Christian Doctrine, Serra Clubs, Councils of Catholic Men and Women, and all the typical groups found in most parishes and dioceses are examples of Church-sponsored and Church-controlled organizations.

Many of these groups have received an explicit official approval and mandate from the bishop of the diocese and are regarded as Catholic Action groups. Catholic Action, as defined by Pius XI, is the "participation of the laity in the apostolate of the Church's Hierarchy." Such organizations have a special place in the work of the Church and usually have spiritual goals—such as catechetical instruction, bringing fallen-aways back into the Church, practicing the spiritual and corporal works of mercy, and promoting various special works of the Church.

But that is not all there is to the lay apostolate. In his address to the Second World Congress in 1957, Pius XII referred to Catholic Action as "a particular form of the lay apostolate" and noted that it must not "claim a monopoly of the lay apostolate, for along with it there remains the free lay apostolate."

Standing midway between the "free lay apostolate," which we shall discuss later, and official Catholic Action is a development of the past three decades in the United States (and other countries, also)—the specialized apostolates. Outstanding examples of these are the Young Christian Students, Young Christian Workers, and the Christian Family Movement. Some of the Sodality groups are also being formed among professional and business men and some Third Orders seem to be moving in this direction also.

These groups represent a cooperative effort of the clergy and laity to form lay apostles spiritually and intellectually and to arm them with the techniques they will need to act efficiently and effectively in the temporal order, particularly within their own special milieu. They are an attempt to give intensive formation to the laity as well as to make them especially aware of the layman's role in the secular community, in the temporal order. In this case, the clergy and the laity work together to help prepare the layman to do his work in the world.

Many of these groups are also mandated by the bishop of their diocese or have official affiliations with the National

Catholic Welfare Conference through the National Councils
of Catholic Men and Women. Their differentiation, however,
lies in their primary concern with the social order. One of their
major goals is to make their members aware of the social
teachings of the Church and to press their members into action in such important matters as race relations, education,
political and economic life, and international affairs. The
groups themselves do not ordinarily take part in such actions
as lobbying, issuing statements on public affairs, or the like,
but they strive to create a social conscience and consciousness
in their members which will encourage them to take effective
action in the world motivated by the social doctrine of the
Church.

The third form of the lay apostolate is in the temporal order,
where the Church's influence reaches only as far as the individual laymen involved. This includes work in labor unions,
civic, professional, educational, and recreational groups, and
political parties in which dedicated laymen work for the common good of their respective groups and for that of the community at large as well.

This free lay apostolate in our society and culture is perhaps
the most pressing in terms of twentieth century needs. We
must always, of course, have the more official types of the lay
apostolate to ensure that the Church keeps strong and vital
from generation to generation. But today the Church is no
longer incarnate in society, she is no longer a vital force in
the events of our times. In our present secularistic type of
society, the major social institutions are not integrated with
or inspired by Christian values and principles; they are separated into neat little compartments.

It does not take a profound mind to analyze the segmen-
talization of the society in which we live. As it has been said,
our modern society is like a copy of *Time* or *Newsweek* in
which everything has an unrelated place: religion, sports, business, medicine, world affairs, and all the rest.

Each segment of our society is a separate unit, bearing in
the minds of most persons only a superficial relation to the

other segments. Life is too much an actual reflection of the
weekly newsmagazines where when an issue is published without a religion section few people note its absence.

Our culture and our social institutions are not integrated
around a common core of shared religious values. They are
not inspired and held together in a unified whole by a uni-
versally accepted set of religious beliefs. Instead, each institution, whether it be the family, politics, economic life, education, religion or recreation, exists in a kind of parallel series
with religion being, for all practical purposes, just another institution on the same level with the rest.

Thus, when the Church surveys our contemporary society
she sees a compartmentalized, segmented kind of world in
which, though it is generally respected and tolerated, sometimes even actively promoted, religion is expected to keep its
place in its own compartment and not interfere with the practical everyday functioning of the other compartments. The late
author-cartoonist Ed Willock summed up much of the problem in one of his jingles: "Mr. Business went to Mass; he
never missed a Sunday. Mr. Business went to hell for what
he did on Monday."

The question we must raise is a natural one: What can be
done about such a dangerous and unchristian situation?

And the answer is that the Church must rely on her lay
members to bring Christ into the market place. The only
method by which the Church can find a place in the busy
secular world is through the laymen who belong to both
worlds—religious and secular—through laymen who have a legitimate role to play in both spheres. It is the layman's job to
penetrate the institutions and culture of our secular society
with Christian principles, to make them conform to the rules
of right reason, to make them work for rather than against
the common good.

The only way laymen can do this directly is to play an active role in secular life, to become a part of secular organizations. Because we are of God we must be vital, functioning
members of the Church. But, likewise, because God has also

made us for the City of Man we must immerse ourselves in the world and become a competent part of it.

"The lay apostolate," commented Archbishop Henry J. O'Brien of Hartford, Connecticut, in 1955, "is not one in which the people help the priest do the priest's work. On the contrary, in the real lay apostolate the priest helps the layman do the layman's work. Only the layman has competence in the social apostolate. It is only the layman, and not the priest, who can bring the social teachings of the Church into his union, into the factory, into the political arena. It is only through the layman that these areas can be truly Christianized."

The relationship between the priest and the layman and the various types of the lay apostolate can be made clear through consideration of a common example involving one social institution—marriage.

Every marriage, every family has problems and difficulties, some religious, some temporal (often economic!). A competent priest, with the help of the Holy Spirit and the cooperation of the people involved, could indeed help the laity (married couple) involved to solve their religious problems. But for the priest, as a priest, to attempt to solve their temporal problems would not only be foolhardy, but possibly dangerous as well. As a priest he would have no competence to provide answers for their financial, personality, or medical problems. Prudence would dictate that he send them to a financial, psychological, or medical counselor for assistance. Religion alone would be no panacea.

Birth control is a particularly apt example. A couple involved in a birth control situation desperately needs the religious help and advice which the priest can give them; they must have the sacraments he administers; they need an understanding of the Church's teaching on birth control and the reasons behind it; and perhaps they must be given an understanding of rhythm. But this is only one feature of the difficulty for many couples. There is another aspect, which the priest is ordinarily unable to cope with directly: the temporal part of the problem. Possibly the reason for the couple's predicament is a low-paying job, an accumulation of debts, inability to find or afford adequate housing, or a host of other possibilities.

This is a segment of the problem that particularly requires lay action in the temporal order, action on the very institutions of society themselves. In order to meet their religious obligations, ordinary people need decent wages, adequate housing, proper medical care, and the whole gamut of physical needs that priests, as priests, are unable to provide for the people coming to them for help.

As recent Popes have repeatedly insisted, laymen have the responsibility to set up the kind of City of Man that will provide these basic minimal necessities. This, the Popes have noted, is primarily a lay responsibility and an area in which laymen are able to take the most direct and effective action. (That they might not always do so is another matter.)

In a way, the example just given highlights and brings to a focus many of the points at issue here. The clergy, as clergy, have no special competence in the temporal order. This is the layman's domain, and the layman can best be helped to do his work by priests who understand this basic premise. The priest who mistakenly believes that the possession of Holy Orders gives him competence in both areas will hinder rather than help the lay apostolate.

These are hard words and it is difficult to say them without appearing to be anticlerical. Fortunately, the same words have been said, and often, by a growing number of the clergy who recognize the necessity for this truth to be understood, lest the lay apostolate never really get off the ground. To recognize that the priest has, by virtue of his ordination, no special competence in the temporal order is not to exclude the clergy from secular life. We have but to look around to be struck by the fact that many of our priests and religious are far more competent in knowledge about the temporal order than are many laymen.

But this competence springs not from their ordination or their religious vows but from special training and education or a superior intellect—natural endowments or accomplishments all. And in the ordinary course of events the well-trained and intellectually competent layman can often accomplish more for the establishment of a just society than the priest with equally valid credentials, simply because the priest is not a member of the temporal order, of the workaday world, in the same way that a layman is.

At a meeting of priests and laymen discussing this problem, Msgr. Daniel M. Cantwell, chaplain of the Chicago Catholic Council on Working Life, explained it this way: "To the laity directly belongs the responsibility for the economic, social, political and cultural spheres of human life. All things belong to God, but not all things are the direct responsibility of the priest. God has given the ordering of temporal life to the laity. In this area, the priest has second place—he is assistant to the people." The priest's principal task, said Msgr. Cantwell, "is to give inspiration to the laity, to energize and stimulate them by his example."

Auxiliary Bishop Floyd L. Begin of Cleveland told the same meeting that "the sooner we are willing to trust laymen to fulfill serious religious and social duties, the sooner we will accomplish the will of God in society. It will never be done by priests alone. . . . Christ never intended this Church to be a priests' Church. Every single man and woman in it has an active part to play—an apostolic mission."

At the same meeting, during the discussion, some points were made which help clear up the relationship between the priest and the layman and the layman's role. One view discussed at length held that the priest was like a member of the general staff of an army who decided on the goals and objectives of the infantrymen (laymen) and picked the targets for the artillery and generally ran the show. The discussion went on for some time until finally a layman who had been sitting quietly the whole time asked for the floor.

"I was a front-line infantryman for four years during the war," he said, "and if you want to use the example you've been using you ought to qualify it a little. One thing an infantryman has to learn is to think for himself and to make his own decisions. Before the battle you can sit around making preparations and looking at the map and choosing goals and objectives. Your officers can see in advance that you are well trained and they can give you pep talks to keep morale high.

"But once the battle begins and you are in the lines the members of the general staff are too far away to tell you what to do. They may have trained you, but when the battle is on you have to decide how to use that training. You may even see that the goals have to be changed or new objectives sought first. Unless a good deal is left to the initiative and ingenuity of the front-line soldiers who are fighting the battle and who know firsthand what the situation is you can easily lose the battle and the war too."

It was not necessary for him to say any more for those present to see the application to the lay apostolate.

Pius XII minced no words when he summed it up for the Second World Congress: ". . . the relations between the Church and the world require the intervention of lay apostles. The *consecratio mundi* [consecration of the world] is essentially the work of the laymen themselves, of men who are intimately a part of economic and social life and who participate in the government and in legislative assemblies. In the same way, only the workers themselves can establish the Catholic cells which must be created among workers in every factory and bring back to the Church those who have strayed from her.

"In this matter ecclesiastical authorities should apply the general principle of subsidiarity and complementarity. They should entrust the layman with tasks that he can perform as well or even better than the priest, and allow him to act freely and exercise personal responsibility within the limits set for his work or demanded by the common welfare of the Church."

Or, as Pope John XXIII put it in 1961 in his great social encyclical *Mater et Magistra*, the Church makes her impact on society "through her lay sons, who should thus feel pledged to carry on their professional activities as the fulfillment of a duty, as the performance of a service in internal union with God and with Christ and for His glory."

The lay apostolate, then, as broadly conceived by the popes and bishops aims especially at the Christianization of society, the natural environment of the layman. Sometimes acting separately, sometimes through organizations; usually acting in their own milieu, according to their gifts and talents, and in cooperation with the clergy, the goal of the apostolic layman is to bring Christ and Christian principles to the world.

Let us not deceive ourselves. To fulfill our role as apostolic laymen in these history-making times will take work. To be effective and efficient, we must work hard and study—especially the social teachings of the Church—to learn what kind of society Christ wants in the world, to learn the goals toward which we must strive as His missionaries. Christ asks much, but He gives abundantly in return when we strive to bring Him into the world.

You may work in a factory. Or an office. Or maybe you're a housewife. Or a mother whose day is taken up with wiping little noses, changing diapers, cooking meals, and doing the family washing and ironing.

You may do any of these things. But you're much more than a factory or office worker, a housewife or mother.

You are Christ's hands and feet in the twentieth century. You're His representative in the factory, the office, the kitchen. Rather than to be present visibly everywhere Himself, He chooses to depend on you, to let you carry Him into every part of this unchristian world.

You are Christ to the world. The Church—the Mystical Body—is depending on you to bring Christ with you wherever you are: in your family circle, in the classroom, the union, the chamber of commerce, the factory, the medical or legal association, the office or smoke-filled political rooms. Christ has willed that, as a member of His Mystical Body, you serve as His personal representative wherever you may be. Through you, He wants to make your little or large segment of the globe His own. He is depending on you.

He has given you a job to do which even His chosen ones, His bishops, priests and religious, cannot perform. They cannot go into your factory or office or kitchen and daily make the spirit of Christ live there. That is your job. Only you can do it.

The bishops and the priests have their own work to do: To administer the sacraments. To inspire, form and train the laity. To show the laity the problems and to help them see their responsibility to solve the problems.

But they can't go out and do your job themselves. Only you can do that. If you won't do it, it won't get done.

CHAPTER 2

The New Look in Clergy-Lay Relations

The results of the current emphasis on the role of the layman in the Church are like the concentric circles created when a pebble is dropped into a quiet pond. One circle causes another in a seemingly never-ending succession of changes.

And like the pebble the lay apostolate is causing many ripples within the structure and function of the Church in America. Not the least of these is a changing relationship between the clergy and the laity, a change which is just beginning to be felt now, but which certainly foreshadows much more of the same in the future.

Of course, it should not really be too surprising that changes are taking place and will continue to do so, for Holy Mother Church herself has been largely responsible for them. Like the good mother she is, she has read the signs of the times for two generations and has been hastening to train laymen for their special job in the Church and the world at a time when Christian influence is desperately needed in society.

To understand where we are today, we must first understand why. And this requires some knowledge of the more recent developments in the status and role of laymen.

Some observers trace our modern situation back to the time of Pope St. Pius X who, earlier this century, emphasized the work of the Confraternity of Christian Doctrine; in some places at least the CCD has grown into an important modern-day training ground for the lay apostolate. But for all practical purposes the beginning of the present changing situation may be dated from the reign of Pope Pius XI, the Pope of Catholic Action, who insisted that laymen play an active role in the reconstruction of the social order.

In a way, it might be said also that the Great Depression of the 1930s was in itself a kind of midwife of the lay apostolate as it was reborn in this century. For during those years when men were face to face with hard reality many of them turned to the Church for answers to their questions—and found them in the rich store of the Church's social doctrine. It was during this era that many Catholic lay groups began to flourish: the labor-school movement, Catholic Worker groups, the Catholic interracial movement, Young Christian Students and Young Christian Workers, plus a variety of others that came and went with the advent of the Second World War.

After the war, many of the older groups remained in existence, but their effect was felt in other ways through their "graduates." Young men and women who had been active in student and worker groups helped form the Cana Conferences and the Christian Family Movement. Still others took their place in the civic community, in politics, and in other forms of public service.

Even today the work continues. The priests who have been associated with the lay apostolate for many years continue to preach the apostolate through the universities or groups with which they are associated. Some of them have become pastors or bishops with the passage of years and within their spheres of influence they promote the interest of laymen in their missionary role. Lay groups themselves continue to turn out well-instructed laymen. And in recent years the National Councils of Catholic Men and Women have been revitalized and, through their programs and publications, stress lay leadership and help provide a vital training ground for it.

Because of all this activity and perhaps most of all because of the encouragement given by Pope Pius XII and many bishops we have entered into what has come to be called the "Age of the Laity." But no new age comes into existence without certain birth pangs; we are now at the stage when clergy and laity are looking at each other and asking, "What comes next?"

And the answer is that two changes come next—one affecting the clergy and the other the laity.

In many respects, at least at first, the changes are going to be much harder on the laity than on the clergy. For the laity have been accustomed for many years to "let Father do it." And the truth is that, even when laymen wanted to do it, Father often did it anyway. So at least the laymen who are middle-aged or older will have to adopt a whole new attitude toward their religious responsibilities in the future. They are, in many ways, like the citizens of newly formed nations who have just won independence from a colonial power. They are not quite sure of their freedom yet and even less certain of how to use it.

Yet, slowly but surely, pastors, either willingly or through force of circumstances—such as the shortage of religious vocations—are turning more and more to their parishioners for assistance. The layman who was seldom called on in the past save for fund-raising is now asked to take part in a diocesan-wide religious census, to help set up a convert course for prospective converts or to help instruct children in their Faith during Sunday-school classes. At the very least in most parts of the country he is asked to participate more fully in the Mass and other of the Church's religious services.

Further, the layman is being reminded of his duties toward the civic community and his responsibilities to act as a Christian in reaching solutions for problems of integration, housing, labor-management relations, and other community questions. Before he can act effectively as a Catholic he must know what the Church teaches and why; this necessitates long hours in discussion clubs, Catholic Action groups, and the reading of numerous books and magazines.

This is one side of the coin.

On the other is the story of younger single and married lay people who have had a taste of the full Christian life either through their education or activity in an apostolic Catholic organization. They have learned to appreciate the meaning of the Mass more, through participation in dialogue Masses or in congregational singing of the Mass. They may have had the opportunity to enjoy and be inspired by energetic young—and old—priests who preach the Mystical Body of Christ, the need for more lay participation in the public prayer of the Church and the place of the layman in the apostolate.

Then these people come back from college to their home parish. Or, the high rate of mobility being what it is in the United States, they move from a modern active suburban parish into an "old-fashioned" one. There they are required to be very silent partners at Mass. Their pastor may not encourage them to take part in the work of the Church in the parish. There might not be any apostolic groups available for them to join with others of like mind.

To put it as mildly as possible, this leaves many of today's younger Catholics frustrated. They know the theory of the lay apostolate. They want to accept their responsibilities as parishioners and as members of the larger community. They want to live the full life of the liturgy as they have come to know it. But on all sides they seem to see disinterest and possibly even disapproval. Or—worse for them in view of their education and previous experience—the only approved groups in their parish may be those in which the pastor or an assistant comes to the meetings only to lecture them or give them all the "answers."

"To attend such meetings," one mature and apostolic Catholic layman with an excellent education told me, "is an insult to my intelligence." He recalled: "I attended as many meetings as I could, but my questions were discouraged and after a while so was I."

"I don't know what to do about our pastor," a young laywoman commented to me on one occasion. "When my husband and I and several other couples went to him for permission to start a family group in our parish he told us we had enough to do to rear our own families and that we shouldn't get involved with other things."

After an article of mine urging increased lay activity appeared in a national Catholic publication, a woman wrote me:

"You've got it all wrong. The problem isn't for lay people to get interested in doing things. I've been trying for five years to get any number of groups going in my parish, but my pastor has turned thumbs down on all of them."

Does all this herald the approach of an incipient anticlericalism on the fringes of the lay apostolate?

I have asked this question specifically of dozens of lay men and women in almost every part of the nation and received everything from incredulous looks to flat denials.

In its classic form, anticlericalism is a hatred of the priesthood and the religious vocation in itself. As a friend who was once a student in a foreign nation remarked: "It is the kind of thing that makes anticlericalists in that country go out of their way in the street car or in a crowd to step on the bare toes of the sandaled monks."

"You have to make a distinction between anticlericalism and impatience," a dedicated layman active in many Catholic organizations told me. "It is hard," he said, "for the layman who has belonged to an apostolic group with sympathetic priests to move into a parish or a city, as I recently had to do, where the pastor and his assistants follow the more traditional approach of the layman in his passive place being told what to do with no respect for his thoughts or opinions.

"But as dissatisfied as I am with their attitudes, I don't dislike them for this. The fact is that my pastor is a sincere priest who gives totally of himself for his people. And so are his assistants. But I am still very impatient that they don't seem to appreciate the role of the layman as much as I think they should, and I'm going to continue to do everything I can to change their views."

Another layman from a different part of the country snorted when I put the question of anticlericalism to him. "I learned early in my brief career in the Army to distinguish between the man and his uniform. And I think that every layman I'm acquainted with knows how to do this. As much as we may disagree with specific priests there is never any question of making a distinction between his views as a man and as a priest."

A priest who is an internationally known scholar commented to me: "You never have anticlericalism without having clericalism first." Fortunately for the Church in America, clericalism has never been a predominant characteristic of our religious life and practices.

This is not to say that tensions and conflicts do not exist; indeed, they do. From the laity's standpoint probably the greatest difficulty is caused by what one priest-editor has called "the omnicompetent priest." This kind of cleric is found in all strata of clerical society; he feels sure of himself in all areas of action and discussion—even those areas where qualified and expert laymen may have some reservations about his judgments.

Of course, the formation of such clerics is easily understandable. As a group, American Catholics are docile and most respectful toward the clergy. In a social group, they always ask for Father's opinion on most any subject and the temptation is as great for the clerical Father to fall into a habit of pontificating as it is for the father of the family to do so with his young children.

This is not infrequently a source of tension for the young, intellectually alert, and educated layman who finds it difficult to accept Father's authority in any but purely ecclesiastical matters and even then if he is rather well read he may on occasion be tempted to raise theological questions for the young priest which do not admit of easy answers. On the surface, at least, most conflict is avoided because of the great respect for the priest, which is characteristic of our culture. In the long run, however, occasional healthy and open disagreements might well prove to be a useful cathartic for clergy-lay relations rather than a continual repression on the part of the laity of their real feelings.

But if the layman has problems making the adjustment to the new relationship that is arising between priest and layman in the United States, so does the priest.

As the younger layman can become impatient with the older priest who does not seem to understand the layman's role, so can the younger priest become discouraged by an often apathetic laity. The priest can work hard to initiate apostolic groups in the parish, to preach the gospel of lay responsibility, and to attempt a more full participation of the laity in the Mass and the sacraments. But too frequently he will have all his efforts fall on deaf ears, on the ears of a laity which have long been conditioned and trained to have Father handle the religion business all by himself.

This is a great trial for many bishops and priests who fully understand what the layman could and should be doing and yet have to learn to be patient in undertaking the lengthy and time-consuming job of educating the next generation to accept its new role. This is not always an easy job when the men of the parish will show up for a meeting in numbers exceeding the usual handful only when a sports movie and proper refreshment is offered to entice them from their television sets.

On a more personal level, there is one change affecting the priest which deserves some extended comment.

At one time in the history of the Church in America the priest in the parish had a kind of double status in the eyes of his parishioner—as a priest and as an educated man. Even only a generation ago, the pastor would likely be one of the few college-educated men in his parish. As a result, his prestige was buttressed by the fact that he was not only a priest of the Church, but likely the best-educated man in the parish as well. Today, the situation has changed, thanks largely to the GI Bill.

Nowadays, a large percentage of any big-city parish is often made up of college graduates; in new suburban parishes the percentage is especially high. As more and more laymen are graduated from college and graduate school with advanced degrees, the priest may find that his work will become more difficult in some ways.

For one thing, apart from his theological training, his relationship with laymen is more and more becoming that of equals; and when the layman is a highly successful and well-educated individual the average priest might well feel ill at ease in his company once the conversation gets away from religion or the trivialities of sports and the weather. The simple truth is that seminary training is not always noted for its cultivation of the arts and sciences; and the priest who does not keep up with these natural conversational areas often feels uncomfortable with a well-read and intelligent layman.

This is especially true in discussion groups and apostolic organizations that discuss the relationship of religion to many phases of modern life. Here the priest is accepted as priest, but he has to prove himself as a conversationalist and as someone who is knowledgeable about world affairs and current events generally. It is simply not easy for the average priest in the typical busy parish to find time, after devoting a couple of hours a day to his Mass, his breviary, and his private prayers to read at least some of the current novels and best-sellers.

The status of the priest is safe on the level of his priesthood; the loyal Catholic layman unquestioningly accepts this. But there is also the role of the educated man, which he must play, often under a severe handicap due to the very nature of his total dedication to the work of his parish.

But this new relationship of the priest and the educated laity as equals and partners in the tackling of mutual problems affecting society and the Church has a bright side. If anything, it is the greatest hope of a better and more effective working arrangement between priest and layman. For already there are indications, based on the experience since World War II that this new situation is working for the mutual benefit of each.

The humble priest who recognizes the special training and competence of individual laymen earns their allegiance and added respect for the priest's own special role. As it has worked out in practice, the priest benefits from a closer acquaintanceship with the realities of everyday life, and the laity learn to appreciate the theological training of the priest more. Each has something to give the other and frequently this cross-fertilization has led priests to read and learn more widely in the area of secular studies and the layman to dip into theological tomes he may never have thought of looking at before.

Of course, this ideal situation is not as yet widespread. There still is what some people call a "cultural lag" between the directives and desires of the Church on the highest levels and the actual implementation of them on the local, parochial scene. This is to be expected, if not always easily accepted.

Yet, after studying the matter at length and discussing it with priests and lay people from all kinds of parishes and situations, I believe the future is tinged with hope. The problems will probably never disappear, certainly at least not for the next one or two generations. But there is a new spirit abroad today among larger and larger numbers of priests and lay people which was not evident even a generation ago. At times things may seem to be changing much too slowly, but the fact remains they *are* changing—and for the better usually.

Perhaps the crux of the matter was caught most delicately by the French theologian, Yves Congar, O.P., in his book, *Laity, Church and World*. Father Congar notes: ". . . it is quite certain that, when lay people are kept in tutelage and treated more or less as children, they become as indifferent to the Church's faith as to her life." And he documents this by telling of a priest who secretly entered Norway a century after the Reformation only to find that the average Catholic didn't even know he was no longer a Roman Catholic. He had come to expect the clergy to run religious affairs so that when changes were made in his worship he just accepted the changes without question.

Father Congar comments that "The good health of the Church requires that the faithful be active, even if (as we see in families and schools) robustly healthy children are a bit more difficult to keep in hand than those who are ailing and spiritless."

In proportion to the health of the lay apostolate in our nation, to that extent will there be difficulty on the part of ecclesiastical authorities to run many of the Church's affairs unilaterally. As more and more is expected and required of laymen, they will undoubtedly respond; but they will also expect and request more and more of a responsible and legitimate voice in the Church.

Accordingly, a great deal of mutual patience and forebearance is going to be required of both clergy and laity in the immediate future. Happily, priests and lay people are beginning to learn to live with each other as a new relationship begins to develop. As a respected bishop wrote me in a private letter not so long ago: "There was a time when I feared the layman, but experience has taught me that he can be mature and trusted."

This is indicative of the new respect and cooperation characterizing the clergy-lay relationship. It will come more slowly in some parts of the country than in others. In some dioceses circumstances have forced the use of more and more laymen because of the shortage of priests and religious and the enormous challenge facing the Church there. And in some others a traditional permissive attitude established a generation ago is now bearing its own fruit in a whole new generation of energetic and intelligent lay people who are taking the ball and running with it at a time when such action is needed more than ever before.

Unfortunately, there are some places where the layman is still regarded as a passive object of the Church's ministrations, pictured in the minds of many in a kneeling and listening position or—as some will have it—with his hand in his pocket. But even in these places, despite the attitude which exists on some of the higher levels, there is, in fact, a change taking place among the laity themselves, who are working quietly, but not ineffectually, for changes in the existing situation.

As we look to the future and see the growing respect and cooperation of clergy and laity for each other, perhaps the thing to keep uppermost in our minds are the words of Pius XII:

"The basic requirement in apostolic work is the most cordial understanding between priests and laity. The apostolate of one is not in competition with that of the other."

CHAPTER 3

Laymen without Voices

The ancient and the new within the Church have been combined in mid-century America to produce a paradox—articulate laymen without voices.

In its crudest form, the problem might be stated this way: The Church has dedicated herself to the education of the laity and now she has a better-educated and better-trained laity than ever before. The Church has likewise encouraged the lay apostolate and she now has a large group of informed and alert lay men and women eager to be of service. But now what does she do with them?

These men and women represent a new force within the Church. They are not rebellious or seeking power; quite the contrary. But they represent a growing reservoir of brains and talent that deserve to be—and indeed must be—utilized in the service of the Church. Yet, there are no clear-cut channels through which their voice may be heard, through which they may prudently and humbly exert a beneficial pressure on the Church.

This difficulty was probably never more apparent than in the preparations for the Ecumenical Council. In Europe, serious attention was given relatively early to enlisting the co-operation of the laity in making the Council as fruitful as possible. Early in 1961, for example, Francis Cardinal Koenig, Archbishop of Vienna, said that lay people should make known their hopes and fears about the coming Council and not stand by as idle witnesses. The cardinal, a member of the Central Preparatory Commission for the Council, told a meeting of Austrian newsmen:

"Do not wait for the Bishop or a report from Rome, if you

have something to say about the Council. Sound a warning whenever you feel you ought to. Urge, when you feel urging is necessary. Wherever the possibility exists, inform the world and Catholics about the Council. Report everything that the people and the Catholics expect concerning the Council."

Even before this, the bishops of Holland had issued a joint pastoral letter in the form of a thirty-page booklet about the Council which spoke especially about the role of the laity. The pastoral letter invited the laity to take up the role of critic of the Church in our times. It pointed out that criticism "as a right and duty of the faithful is an expression of love—a love that only with reluctance points out the mistakes of its mother, a love that carefully seeks, moreover, with a Christian tact, for the best possible means of making known its filial observations and remarks, a love, finally, that does not undermine its own adherence or that of others to the Faith."

During this period, at a general audience, Pope John pointed out that "The apostolate of the laity, which aids the priest in spreading the kingdom of God, has had an enormous development in modern times. It is now being given detailed consideration and will be for the fathers of the Council an object of vital concern and special study."

Coincidentally, a few days after these stories were published, I had occasion to meet socially with a small group of outstanding Catholic laymen. Some of them were authors of books, others were professors, lecturers, journalists—men of stature in their professions and in the practice of their Faith. I commented on what the Holy Father had said and raised the question implied by the Dutch bishops and by Cardinal Koenig's statement: "What do you think about the Council and how would you go about passing your thoughts on to the ecclesiastical authorities?" The first reaction of these gentlemen was that I was trying to amuse them. After they had ascertained that this was not true, two facts became immediately apparent.

One was that no one present had ever entertained the slightest thought of making his feelings about the Council known, even though most of them were experienced men with considerable work in various forms of the lay apostolate.

The other fact was that none of them had any clear idea of how they would proceed to make their thoughts felt if they wanted to do so. After some group consideration, a number of tentative suggestions were made—writing their bishop, bringing up the subject in lectures or articles so it would receive public attention, finding out who was in charge of a particular Council commission and then writing him. The point to note, however, is that none of these above-average men was *sure* of how to proceed.

Almost before I had a chance to think through my own reaction to this incident, another news story came along with added interest. Martin Work, executive director of the National Council of Catholic Men, had just returned from Rome and he commented that the lay people of the United States were lagging behind in proposing suggestions regarding the lay apostolate for the Vatican Council.

Mr. Work, the only American member of the Permanent Committee for International Congresses of the Lay Apostolate, commented further: "The laity of Europe are much more articulate in making suggestions to the proper ecclesiastical authorities to be placed before the Ecumenical Council regarding the lay apostolate. . . . It appears evident that the Council authorities would welcome expressions from lay organizations."

The problem of the Council is an important, but a passing one for the lay people of America. It is only part of a much broader problem—a difficulty that is perhaps best summarized under the general heading of "Freedom of Speech within the Church."

Whatever the problem may be in Europe, I believe that in the United States it is the twofold one hinted at by my experience with my lay friends: there is no tradition in the Church in America of "free speech" for the laity; and there is no structure existing in the official Church for communication between the laity and the clergy and hierarchy (or, indeed, in many instances between the clergy and the hierarchy, though this is not our concern here).

It is quite understandable, of course, why "free speech" is a Johnny-come-lately problem for us. The American Church as a whole is barely out of the brick-and-mortar stage (and is still in that stage in some parts of the nation). The Irish and the Germans and Poles and Italians who made up the great Catholic immigrations to America were not, as a group, from scholarly backgrounds. Their faith and piety were firm and well grounded, but they were so occupied erecting most of the churches in which we now worship that, apart from isolated instances, they had no time to worry about the matter of communication.

It is only now that the sons, grandsons, and great-grandsons of these immigrants have attained the position in which a difficulty arises. And the Church herself is largely responsible. For years the Church has expended great energy in educating a more mature and responsible laity. In more recent times, she has concentrated on the formation of a lay elite. Now she has the beginning of a significant pool of intelligent and educated lay people. How is she to utilize them most effectively and efficiently?

Within the framework of the problem of "free speech," I think the alternatives are clear: the Church must set up some structure through which they may be heard or she must be prepared to face the problem of losing her investment in the education of the laity.

Do not misunderstand, I do not fear rebellion on the part of the laity. I fear apathy. In two decades of various kinds of association with many forms of the lay apostolate, I have met a broad cross section of lay people and I have yet to meet one who was really a rebel against the Church. I have encountered some who were impatient or imprudent or youthful radicals, but not rebellious. And I have come across others a decade or two later who had lost interest, who had become apathetic. They had become tired of knocking their heads against the solid door of endless no's, maybe's, and "We'll look into it." But even these did not lose their faith, although some no longer possessed the lively interest which once characterized them.

Apart from any theological overtones or ramifications, the problem is basically one of good administration. No union leader or business executive or ecclesiastic can supervise a smoothly running operation without keeping his communications pipelines open. Now, I am the first to admit that the parish priest or religious superior or bishop has the not inconsiderable assistance of the Holy Spirit to aid him. But I would still maintain that this is no substitute for also using every worth-while human device to achieve the success of a project, human or divine.

And it is difficult to overestimate the value and importance of a specific kind of social structure to handle the problem of communications from the laity. For example, if a layman moves into a new parish, he knows how to go about registering. Or if he wants to marry or to obtain a legal divorce he also is aware that certain steps must be taken by his pastor to handle this situation. But if he wants to carry on some communications with his pastor or his bishop as a loving critic, to paraphrase the Dutch bishops, neither he nor his pastor nor, perhaps, the bishop knows how to deal with such a situation, for this kind of situation is simply not provided for within the present framework of the Church. There is no set way of going about it with the rights and duties and channels all predetermined so it can be expedited with a minimum of friction. At least there is no set way of dealing with this in the same sense that a union steward knows how to proceed in the case of a grievance or a personnel manager in handling an issue in terms of set company policy.

It does seem a waste to overlook the great wealth of data available to us in the area of human relations from the monumental studies which have been made in the fields of industrial sociology and industrial psychology. All of these studies agree that production and morale are intimately related: when morale is high, production is high. Of course, one of the indispensable conditions of high morale is for the members of a work (or other) group to feel they are an integral part of the production process, that they are depended on, that their skills, their abilities, their opinions are valued and will be listened to.

In terms of communication within the Church, I believe this has many practical and concrete applications.

Most parishioners I know, for instance, want to have a say in the conduct of their parish. Not, mind you, in the things that pertain exclusively to the work of the pastor, but in the many vital areas of parish life which directly affect them: the hours for confessions and Mass; the amount of tuition in the school; the procedures followed in fund drives; participation in the Mass; the work of parish societies; the running of the parish school.

I am sure that any American Catholic layman could easily volunteer an unhappy story of tension that developed in his parish because one of these aspects of parish life was decided arbitrarily, without adequate care being given to the needs and desires of the parishioners. Yet, how easy it is to avoid such problems.

I have always admired the wise pastor I heard about who was on the verge of building a new parish church. He had two sets of plans, equally adequate in terms of financing, decoration, and the rest. He favored one heavily himself, but he let the members of his parish vote for the final choice. They voted overwhelmingly against him. Master of human relations that he was, he allowed their vote to decide the matter, thus precluding the years of petty ill will that inevitably would have arisen had he gone ahead to follow his own tastes.

Not so happy was the story told me by a layman—a story which is, I fear, increasingly typical as the high cost of operating a parochial school becomes even higher. The layman in question is a convert, docile and obedient; he is sold on the Church and whatever she says is good enough for him.

Yet, he was thoroughly shaken by a difficult experience at the final parent-teachers meeting of one school year.

The bishop of his diocese had announced that there would be no tuition charged in the schools of the diocese in the future, on the grounds that the school was a responsibility of the entire parish, not just of the parents whose children were enrolled. Accordingly, the PTA meeting was discussing financial plans for the coming year. For his part, the pastor suggested that the parents sponsor a number of dances during the school year to raise money for tuition and various other school needs.

The president of the PTA, an experienced economist, asked if the school budget had been set for the next year so that the parents and others in the parish could make financial plans as to how much would be expected of them. The pastor pointed out that he had no budget and was not accustomed to using one; he noted that he could rely on "special collections" if necessary.

With a feeling that they had a great contribution to make, the president of the PTA as well as several businessmen present volunteered to help the pastor prepare a budget to make the parishioners' financial responsibility clear as well as to consider the possibility of raising additional money for more and more well-qualified lay teachers—who were badly needed.

Unfortunately, the parishioners were not entirely prepared for the pastor's stern rejection of their idea to tamper with the operation of *his* school and to raise the ugly specter of trusteeism in *his* parish!

When he related the story to me, the layman was still somewhat in a state of emotional depression. He had been listening to the pleas for a more active laity; this was his first venture, as a Catholic, to be of assistance to his parish and, furthermore, he didn't even know what trusteeism was.

Although most people probably share this layman's ignorance of trusteeism, they will likely be hearing more and more about it for it is a kind of scare word for many pastors and in its own way it will undoubtedly cause frequent conflicts or at least arouse tensions increasingly in the future. The main point to be considered is that some lay trustees during the earlier days of the Church in America interfered with the administration of the Church and in some parishes and dioceses caused considerable dissension. As a result, there has been a natural tendency on the part of clerics to avoid giving lay people too much control in parochial life, particularly over the purse strings.

Yet, the historical context has changed drastically since the trusteeism troubles and so have the needs of the Church. It hardly seems desirable to cut the laymen off almost completely from effective help in the parish, particularly in the management of purely temporal affairs in which he has a personal stake, just to avoid the remote possibility of some difficulty. After all, it would not be a difficult matter to take adequate precautions to prevent a recurrence of trusteeism. But it will be increasingly difficult to tell lay people that they are important in the life of the parish and request their help and, on the other hand, to rebuff them when they offer aid where it is likely most needed. This is particularly so in view of the shortage of religious vocations. As my friend remarked, "Why should my pastor have to waste so much time with finances and running the school when there are dozens of people in the parish who badly need his spiritual help and guidance?" Why, indeed, is the question more and more lay people are asking.

Unless there is a mutual respect and desire to serve and be of service existing between pastor and parishioner it seems quite likely that morale and "production" will not remain consistently at the optimum level. There are a multitude of decisions which must be made in every parish from week to week that do not involve principle or doctrine but, rather, matters in which the parishioners have a considerable interest. Apart from the fact that most parishes have not done so in the past, why should not the parishioners be consulted and involved in the making of decisions intimately affecting them and their children?

On the diocesan level, the problem becomes more complex. Obviously, the amount of communication is going to vary drastically between, for example, a metropolitan see on the

East Coast and a more or less missionary diocese in the Southwest. But communication is still a vital problem. In either case, the pastor is a key link in passing on the thinking of his people, but diocesan-wide organizations of the laity also have an important function.

Here, because different levels are involved, different approaches might be used. The diocesan newspaper could well serve as a channel of communication both ways—from the bishop to his people, and from the people to the bishop. Father Rahner notes, in his book *Free Speech in the Church*:

"Divine though the Church may be in origin—in her constitution and doctrine, her sacraments and her law—she has an earthly existence too: she has her own . . . forms of spirituality, liturgy, care of souls, moral behavior, administration, societies, organizations, etc., which to some extent, though not exclusively, express the fluctuating, predominantly natural conditions of the day. The Church has always to be adapting her actual existence to contemporary conditions. . . ."

Becoming more specific, he says: "In our own day, for instance, there can be open discussion as to whether there would be some point in a reform of the Breviary, or even whether there should be a modification of the Mass itself. . . . Would it have been such a bad thing if a few words could have been found occasionally in Catholic newspapers [in the past] on the subject of the awful complexity of the rules about fasting before Holy Communion, which have not always seemed to preserve the real spirit of this ordinance of the Church? . . . Are there not large groups of people amongst what is on the whole a fairly loyal body of laymen who privately deplore many of the educational methods in use in Catholic institutes and monastic establishments and yet never say a word about it in public—and never will, wrongly imagining that they never may?

"The fact is that reforms of this kind naturally often need the pressure of public opinion if they are not to be stifled by tradition. Even in the higher reaches of the Church, people can believe that all is well because no complaints and wishes

for any sort of change have been heard, or because if they have
they seem to be simply isolated views with no weight of
public opinion behind them."

It should be noted that Father Rahner is writing, not as a
radical, but as a widely known and respected theologian; the
words of his book are couched in the most cautious of terms
and every statement is qualified, as you would expect in the
work of a professional student of theology.

And he puts a heavy burden on the layman to know what
the Church says and teaches and to make the life of the
Church his own; he demands that the layman should be at
least as well instructed in his religion as he is in secular fields
of knowledge. His words give no comfort to the Sunday
morning quarterback who feels it a duty to discuss at great
length with his fellow parishioners the real and imagined faults
of his pastor.

On the contrary, as Father Rahner says: "Ultimately it all
boils down to the fact that every individual Christian is responsible in his own day and way for the Church and the life
of the Church."

There is no single or easy solution for these multitudinous
problems of "free speech" and communication which now face
the Church in the United States and which will, without a
doubt, get worse before they get better. But it is imperative
that the problem be faced up to now, before it grows to any
greater proportions, and that it be worked out according to the
individual needs of each parish and diocese.

The laity will never "revolt," but it would be a tragedy to
have the unparalleled enthusiasm and mature experience of
lay people today lost for lack of a legitimate means of expressing their opinions. To avoid such a possibility it is urgent that
we begin now to consider the formation of a tradition of "free
speech." One way or another, voices must be found for the
Catholic laymen of America.

CHAPTER 4

Lay Life with God

Along with the increasing interest in the role of the layman in the temporal order, there has developed simultaneously considerable theorizing about the spiritual life most suited for the modern layman. There are those, for example, who say that we cannot even speak of "lay" spirituality, that it is really like love of God and neighbor, in which the love involved is one reality and not two distinct elements. Spirituality, too, they say, is one and cannot be dissected into separate types for the priesthood, the religious life, and the lay vocation.

Yet, if it is possible to differentiate Benedictine, Carmelite, or Franciscan spirituality, why not a "lay" spirituality? If we describe spirituality as living a life of union with Christ, there is a certain legitimacy in distinguishing the types of lives that may be led in the quest for a deeper and more intimate sharing in the divine life.

True, even two such disparate persons as the factory worker in a metropolitan area and the Trappist in his cloister share one and the same divine life. But their circumstances and the environments which affect them are so radically different that it would be foolhardy to pretend that the dissimilarities are purely accidental.

There is no need, however, to seek out the striking example of differences between a factory worker and a monk. In some ways, there are as many areas of difference between the parish priest in his rectory and the urban office worker across the street surrounded by his wife and family. They, too, both seek union with the Redeemer, but their modes of life are so unlike that it sometimes seems difficult to reconcile them.

Ultimately, we are forced to refine our description of spirituality as living a life of union with Christ *according to our circumstances*. And in this sense we may more easily distinguish the layman's way of life from those of the priest and the religious.

Because of his lay vocation, the average married man, for instance, is faced with three particular sets of circumstances in his search for spirituality—personal, family, worldly.

The search for intimacy with the divine is always basically an individual, personal problem. Though married, the layman still remains alone in many respects. In his marriage, he may find himself more alone at times, if only psychologically, and with more need for self-reliance than when he was single.

Especially in the child-bearing years must he often seek spirituality when his wife is occupied with the children and he with the pursuit of financial stability. The initial union he and his wife shared in participating in the Mass together, for example, most likely will be gone when they have several small children and husband and wife must take turns baby-sitting while one of them goes to Mass. Or if they take their smaller children to Mass they may each spend more time supervising the behavior of their children than in offering the Holy Sacrifice. This, of course, has nothing to do with the objective merit they obtain by their attendance at Mass, but the subjective opportunity to recollect oneself at Mass and achieve personal psychological as well as spiritual refreshment may well be lost for years as their children are growing.

A man's struggle to retain the spiritual practices of his single life becomes more and more difficult—often in direct proportion to the number of children he has. Solitude becomes a problem, as he is practically never alone and has little time for personal devotions, much less for formal meditation or involved study or spiritual reading, which takes time and concentration. And being up several times during the night with the children does not lend itself to springing cheerfully from his couch in the darkness of the morning to attend Mass and receive Holy Communion. Even where he may receive Communion in one of the big city churches on his way to work, a slender budget may make the purchase of breakfast afterward a formidable obstacle that may deter him from enjoying the fruits of the Mass. How many devout men I knew in their earlier years as daily communicants with high ideals have told me in their later years that they regarded the first ten or fifteen years of their marriage as a spiritual blank, a time for which they were unprepared and in which they found it most difficult to come to grips with their new state in life.

Perhaps this picture is painted in too dark a hue. It is true that many couples do not have a large family and even in large families the children do grow up. And many are not too pinched financially. But the point is still valid that marriage and family life profoundly affect the individual in his personal seeking for a deeper and more meaningful union with his Saviour.

Furthermore, spirituality for our hypothetical married layman is not a personal affair alone. He must work out his salvation within the framework of his married and family life. He must help his wife and family develop a conjugal and family spirituality in the midst of a world filled with conflicting and often contradictory values and norms.

The exterior pressures on the family have been incisively described and analyzed by many competent observers of the family unit. But there are many common problems inherent within the family circle which have not often been explored in the context of lay spirituality. Order is one of these problems.

Books on the spiritual life commonly tell us that order and regularity are indispensable for a well-grounded spiritual life. But order and regularity are two factors not often found in the lives of young couples rearing a family. Their lives appear to be ones of organized disorder, with their children plotting at every turn to make each day unlike every other day. In theory, this should create no spiritual problem for married couples. Their life of distraction has been willed for them by God, and so long as they do the best they can, they are doing God's will.

The problem arises in the minds of the couples themselves, however. And it is a problem precisely because of the lack of any widespread teaching or understanding of "lay" spirituality, because spirituality is often confused with the number of prayers said or pious exercises performed.

Couples frequently have the idea that they have no spiritual life and that it is foolish even to attempt to develop one if they are unable to get in all their prayers or at least give some formal conscious thought to God every day. The housewife, for instance, who has fought the battle of her children all day long is ready to drop in the evening when she and her husband finally tuck the last child in for the night. Then, suddenly, she realizes that she didn't say a prayer all day or once think about God since her morning offering.

One couple I knew, typical of many, took their marriage, their vocation, their sanctity seriously from the time they became engaged. During the first months after their wedding, they worked out a neatly wrapped package of the way in which they would build their home on religious practices. They had time set aside each day for at least a little spiritual reading; they said the rosary together daily; they went to Mass and received the sacraments together regularly; they made a married couples' retreat together.

Then came the first baby, and the second, and the third. . . .

That was the end of the well-planned program. As the family grew, the mother complained: "The children take so much time that I even have a hard time getting to Sunday Mass. If I'm not washing diapers, I'm wiping noses, or preparing meals. I barely get the children dressed and out for the morning when they're back in for lunch. When the dishes are washed, I have a little time to get the house straightened out; then it's time to begin supper. There's no such thing as a time to pray or read any more."

Later on, when the children are in school, the mother will find herself caught up in a round of activities. The father, who formerly spent time getting the small children to bed, will have to help with homework or devote time to hobbies and games.

With little understanding of "lay" spirituality, the husband

and wife soon feel spiritually drained, too, and overcome with the feeling that they not only have no spiritual life at all, but that it will be fruitless even to think about it until some future date when the children are all reared.

Of course, a pat answer is to point out that when you are in the state of grace all the distracting activities of family life, if performed from a good motive, bring you closer to Christ. The question is, how to make this theological truth live for the persons concerned?

To continue with the example of the housewife, she must be made to realize that the feeding and clothing, admonishing and instructing of her children are just as much works of mercy as if she had done them for persons outside her family. She must be taught to see Christ in her husband, her children, and her neighbors, to understand that by serving them she is serving her Redeemer.

Further, the Mystical Body must be made a living reality. Parents must be helped to see the profound wealth of meaning it has for their family's spiritual life through an understanding of such statements as that of Pius XII in his encyclical on the Mystical Body (italics added):

". . . the salvation of many depends on the prayers and voluntary penances which the members of the Mystical Body of Jesus Christ offer for this intention, and on the assistance of pastors of souls and of the faithful, *especially of fathers and mothers of families,* which they must offer to our divine Saviour as though they were His associates."

These are the kind of spiritual realities which, once understood, put meat on the bare bones of theological truths. The problem, of course, is to develop priests who understand both theology and family life, who can state the theological profundities in vital terms and concrete examples.

Perhaps needed even more are laymen who know theology, who can bring about a wedding of theology and marriage. I recall attending a national Catholic family life meeting some years ago at which we were discussing these matters and a priest finally commented that the last word on the theology of marriage would probably be said at some future date by a lay theologian with fifteen children.

Of course, the priest who made the statement was not referring to lay theologians in the sense in which it has been condemned, but rather he was pointing out that laymen must not remain totally aloof from theology. Instead, they must more than ever before learn enough about theology so that they can apply it to the complexities of marriage and family life. For the theology of marriage to become most fruitful, priests must understand the practicalities of marriage more deeply and laymen must, in turn, make every effort to understand the truths of theology. Only in this way will a really effective spirituality for married couples be created and sustained.

Straight thinking on the theology of marriage is absolutely necessary if husband and wife are to make any spiritual progress. Occasionally you run into a young married man or woman who, possibly without realizing it, resent the children God has given them. This type of person can miss the ridiculous contradiction in his attitude as he regrets the roadblocks his growing family puts in the way of his spiritual growth. "I'm willing to make the sacrifice," he tells himself, "but it is one of the biggest sacrifices. Things were going so smoothly. I could have made so much progress . . . if I could have continued to concentrate on spiritual values."

Talk about the grass being greener on the other side of the fence! This is the same kind of self-delusion that makes a young religious in the novitiate believe that in six weeks he can get rid of all his vices, in another six weeks he can gain all the virtues, and then he'll be ready for canonization. Actually, this husband or wife has the foolish notion that sanctity becomes more difficult for him because he is following God's will. That's what a vocation is—whether it's a vocation to the priesthood or to marriage—the special kind of life in which God wants us to become a saint. Holiness doesn't come easily for anyone. If it seems to, it would be a pretty good bet that it's not real holiness.

Caring for the twenty-four-hour-a-day demands of small

children is the way most parents are expected to practice the spiritual and corporal works of mercy. Slaving at a desk, a stove, or an assembly line can be just as meritorious for the parent as the missionary's long hours devoted to the care of outcast lepers. Children should not be obstacles to grace any more than Jesus was an obstacle to the sanctity of Mary and Joseph; they should be the occasions for grace. If they are not, it is not the fault of the children; it's the fault of the parents who are feeling sorry for themselves and longing for a life to which God didn't call them.

Christ told us that whatsoever we do for the least of His brethren, we do for Him. Among these "least of His brethren" are our own children. When we feed and clothe the infant, we are serving Christ. When we instruct and discipline the growing child, we are serving Christ. When we advise the teenager and gradually make that painful recognition of his self-reliance, we are still serving Christ. The parent who sees Christ in his children and serves them unselfishly is opening the door of his soul to divine grace and love. He is bringing his own will into conformity with the will of God. This is becoming a saint.

Every state of life has its own particular virtues and opportunities for holiness, and the married state is no exception. Charity—love of God and neighbor—is essential for all, but the mother and father have special opportunities to develop this love in the sympathy, understanding, and sacrifice that is demanded of them as part of the daily routine.

Sacrifice is the only language in which love can express itself, and sacrifice is at the core of marital and family life. Parents must learn to sacrifice their time and their own wishes —constantly—for the common good of their family. In this sense, marriage is "a school of perfection."

Children, simply by being themselves, offer their parents a continuing opportunity for growth in the virtues. Charity, because children sop up love like dry sponges; love is the ground in which the personality of the child can grow. Obedience, because the child's ever-present demand for attention

right now is a constant call for the parents to obey the obligations they accepted when they chose their vocation. Humility,
because the parents are steadily called upon to subject their
wishes, their ambitions to the good of the family. And what
better occasion for humility can you find than the understanding acceptance of the "taken for granted" attitude with
which most children regard their parents and the sacrifices
their parents make for them?

Also, in the work of forming a child's character is a constant
reminder to the mother and father that they must re-examine
their own characters. The father who hears his son begin to
use some of the off-color expressions which he himself uses,
or the mother who hears her teen-aged daughter echoing the
cutting gossip she herself passed on to a neighbor over morning coffee will usually experience a severe jolt. This kind of
lesson will have more effect than a half-dozen sermons on
scandal. Thus, the parents are under a constant pressure to
put into their own lives the virtues they are trying to develop
in their children. The whole pattern of married life lends itself to a realistic, down-to-earth formula for growth in sanctity.
The parents who live up to their obligations for the right motive (to show their love of God) have the battle half-won.

The concrete circumstances of spiritual growth are different
for the married person, for the priest or religious. Sanctity for
the husband or wife grows out of the home and family. For
the priest and religious it must grow out of different surroundings (though the roots and the flower are the same). There is
another difference. The priests and the religious have re-
nounced "the world." Though they devote their lives to the
sanctification of this world, they must not be of it. The married person is part of the world, and this fact, too, will make
his approach to sanctity distinctive.

This brings us to the third area that affects the layman's
struggle for spirituality—his relationship with the world. Here
we shall just touch upon a few basic problems which we shall
explore at greater length in the next chapter.

Laymen cannot try to escape from the world by becoming

indifferent to it. Those who, because of their vocations, live in the world must accept that fact and the world with it. It is, at least in part, through the world that the layman must become holy.

The priest and the religious seek to withdraw from the world, to be in it, but not of it. The authentic layman must embrace the world as his monastery. If he attempts to withdraw, he is playing false to his lay vocation, which is to bring Christ to the world, indeed to be Christ to the world. And this world is not just an extension of personal relationships; it is a vast complex of social systems and cultures to which the layman must bring the Saviour. This does not mean that laymen must give up their own individual, personal prayer lives, but it may well mean, for instance, that it might be the better part to skip spiritual reading one night in order to attend a PTA meeting.

Laymen generally recognize that the way to sanctity is through doing God's will. But most of them have never been instructed beyond the stock mission example of the wife who will please God more by staying home from Mass on a weekday morning in order to make her husband's breakfast. The principle has seldom been broadened to include, for example, civic and community life.

And this is getting close to the heart of the problem—a twofold problem. A full-blown theology of the laity has yet to be developed. And the thinking along these lines that is available has not yet begun to sift down to the laity to any appreciable degree. In practical terms, this means that the average layman must continue to develop his spirituality—for better or worse —on the priestly or religious model. And a watered-down clerical approach to spirituality can at best be only a poor substitute for the laity; it will never fully serve their needs.

In addition, from a social viewpoint, there is a double danger. The laity may either seek to withdraw from the world, leaving it to its enemies, or they may, lacking proper understanding and guidance, become so immersed in it that they will forget their spiritual motivations. The delicate balance requires laymen to involve themselves in the world, but also never to forget their primary purpose, to make that world an extension of the Mystical Body.

Lay people today desperately want and need to know many things beyond their basic understanding of the necessity for a more frequent and more fruitful participation in the Mass and the sacraments. They want to have a full grasp of what their role should be as members of the Mystical Body. They want to know how to reconcile their personal and family spirituality with the demands of the world. They want to know how to organize their lives on a spiritual level in the midst of all their worldly cares and concerns.

In short, lay people want and need to be helped to understand and develop a spirituality suited to their needs as lay people. They must be taught, among other things, that their holiness can develop from an apostolic spirituality that builds on interior sanctity and seeks God through Christianizing the family and the culture and institutions of society.

Laymen must be shown how the liturgy incorporates us into Christ and in what ways it helps us live grace-filled lives close to the Church. Especially must they understand the Mass and such facts, as, for example, that we are not just spectators at the Holy Sacrifice but actors helping to continue the sacrifice of Calvary in time through offering ourselves along with Christ to the Eternal Father.

A generation of spiritually starved lay people are asking for divine bread. Who will give it to them?

CHAPTER 5

The World Is Not Evil

The letter from my layman friend mentioned it in passing: "I was talking to a young priest, recently ordained, who found it almost impossible to understand how human values could be anything but instruments of the life hereafter. . . ."

I kept a copy of the letter to think about because I believe that brief quotation summarized an intriguing new problem for the young, educated American Catholic layman which is going to receive increasing attention in the future. The sentence is a harbinger of a quiet twentieth-century Renaissance now germinating in the fertile soil of the lay apostolate. Basically it all centers around the place of human, temporal values in the life of the Christian, the relationship of the natural to the supernatural, the place of this world in our struggle to reach the next.

Admittedly, the problem is not a new one. At its core it is the ancient discussion all over again, a concern prefigured in the New Testament use of the word *cosmos* and discussed in more recent years as Christian Humanism, which in Father Yves de Montcheuil's words (in his *For Men of Action*) is "a Christian love of the human element."

But the average layman today knows naught of the term Christian Humanism. His problem is one of the practical, concrete order in which he finds himself confronted by a situation he does not always understand and which he probably has never heard described or analyzed. He feels it rather than knows it, although this does not necessarily make it any less real for him.

Historically, the contemporary layman's problem began with the rise of the modern lay apostolate earlier this century.

In broad, general terms, the layman's spiritual concerns for some centuries had been based primarily on the avoidance of evil and to a large extent a withdrawal from secularistic society. The Church, having been badly battered by the Protestant Revolt, was on the defensive and sought to preserve the faith of its members by withdrawing them from the onslaughts of the agnostics and atheists and scientific determinists.

As Msgr. Gerard Philips points out in *The Role of the Laity in the Church*: "In the writings of the New Testament we make no mistake about the meaning of the word *Cosmos*. The sense is twofold: it indicates either the whole of creation and man, or the horde of the enemies of God and His Christ." This latter view of the world seems to have prevailed until well into the twentieth century, thus encouraging many laymen to avoid too much personal contact with new social philosophies or with the vast new scientific and technological world arising around them on the ashes of the Middle Ages.

The spirituality of that period is perhaps best symbolized by the eminently respectable *Imitation of Christ*, which preaches a disdain for the things of the world. Despite its continuing popularity, an increasing number of my fellow laymen and some of the priests I know regard the *Imitation* as anti-intellectual and anti-Christian Humanist. They are concerned because the *Imitation* embodies primarily a monastic spirituality; much of it is especially aimed at the spiritual development and needs of the priest or religious. Indeed, taken literally by the layman who does not have a reasonably extensive knowledge of the spiritual life, it could do harm to persons, to marriages, to the social apostolate of the Church.

The student or the scholar, for example, must know exactly how to understand a statement such as: "At the day of judgment it shall not be asked of us what we have read, but what we have done; not how well we have said, but how religiously we have lived." The salesman—of God or goods—must know exactly how to interpret: "Covet to be familiar only with God and with his angels; but the familiarity of man, as much as thou mayest, look thou eschew." And the Christian who has a love of the fine arts must not develop a guilt complex when he reads: "But if thou take heed to the goodness everlasting, thou shalt well see that these worldly goods and worldly likings are but little worth, and that they be rather more grievous than pleasant. . . ."

Understood properly, the *Imitation* can be very helpful to souls. The problem is that it, and others like it in the traditional approach, concentrate on a personal, to the exclusion of a social or apostolic, spirituality, on the interior life without developing the exterior or "worldly" (in the good sense) life. Such an approach simply does not meet the needs of many of today's laymen who find much more rapport with words such as these from *Christians in the World*, by Father Jacques Leclercq:

"In our times the construction of the kingdom [of God] has assumed different proportions from those of former times. We are living in a world dominated by the problems of social organization. The technical progress of our time makes it possible to establish a social order securing to all men means of development that correspond to the exigencies of human dignity, through instruction, material well-being and the organization of collective life.

"The building up of the kingdom presupposes that Christians should play a part in all this, stirred up by the spirit of Christ, that problems like those of transport, of international cooperation, in education and science as well as in economic matters, should be studied by Christians animated by the spirit of Christ. For this it is essential in the first place that they be animated by this spirit and that Christians should animate Christians in the Church with this spirit; but the object is for Christians to act on the world in such a way that the world becomes more like what a kingdom of God on earth should be and that they, the Christians, should make the purity of such a life appreciated."

This attitude is an excellent barometer of the changing nature of the laity today. And the change itself has come about largely because of the Church herself through the Catholic educational system and the current emphasis on the apostolate of the laity.

When the modern layman began to appear earlier this century, the stress was heavily on the laity assisting the priest in the work of education and the salvation of souls. Then, confronted with the vast changes affecting political and economic society from about the time of the Great Depression onward, the emphasis began to shift. Perhaps more than ever before in modern times laymen were encouraged to play leading roles in the affairs of the world, and Pius XII gave explicit papal approval to this view in his address to the Second World Congress of the Laity when he spoke of the layman's role in the "*consecratio mundi.*"

Father Yves Congar, the French Dominican theologian, also captures some of this new spirit in his classic work, *Lay People in the Church,* when he writes:

"Would it be wrong or exaggerated to say that fresh values are being recommended to the faithful in view of new calls of grace in these times? We are thinking of the many writings which, without for a moment forgetting the law of the Cross, offer Christians a humanist ideal, a candid engagement in earthly activities and a positive view of their worth. We are thinking of the renewed vision of the world of nature, the keen concern about work and the world of work, the interest taken by the clergy in men's real life. We are thinking of the many pronouncements in which the leaders of God's people, and notably Pope Pius XII, declare the goodness of earthly activities, of the body and of sport, of marriage as being in its own way an occasion and means of perfection. We are thinking of that impressive collection of texts in which the Church's pastoral magisterium encourages the faithful to recognize the value of initiative, of strength, of confidence, of cheerful and energetic collaboration in human work and earthly progress. . . . All this is supported by the actual lived experience, not of lukewarm lay people of 'worldly' tendencies, but of those who are very fervent and deeply committed Christians. It is plain that all these things mean something and indicate a current that is being providentially guided in the Church of our time."

Because of all the ferment, which Father Congar so well describes, the lives of American Catholic laymen have been caught up in two mainstreams, which now have carried them to the point where they are faced with the problem of human values. On the one side, the Church herself has been encouraging them to play significant roles in the affairs of the world. And on the other, the modern American Catholic layman has been pushed in the same direction by his changing social status.

His new position in American society has been chronicled many times in recent years. Increased education and concomitant economic success have thrust him into the middle class. He is now beginning to learn to appreciate and respect the middle class pursuits of his neighbors—particularly the fine arts and the good things of life. He and his wife may attend the symphony, the theater, the opera, art show, and the rest. Within his microcosmic existence he is experiencing a kind of renaissance.

As Pope John noted in *Mater et Magistra*, "Today the Church is confronted with the immense task of giving a human and Christian note to modern civilization, a note that is required and is almost asked for by that civilization itself for its further development and even for its continued existence."

This new awakening to the finer things of life, coupled with his Church's insistence that he be concerned with the social and cultural life of his community, has now produced a tension in his life, which will have to be resolved. And whether he realizes it or not, this tension is the problem of Christian Humanism.

On the one hand he is faced with the remnants of the withdrawal-from-the-world school of spiritual life which Father John Courtney Murray in an essay in *Social Order* in 1953 terms eschatological humanism. As Father Murray points out, "the eschatological view lays emphasis on the central truth that Christianity is the Cross. And the Cross represents the inversion of all human values. The human is put to death; and out of the death comes life. . . . Pushed to the extreme, the conclusion would be that man not only may in fact neglect, but even should by right neglect, that which is called the cultural enterprise—the cultivation of science and the arts, the pursuit of human values by human energies, the work of civilization—in order to give undivided energies to the invisible things of the spirit."

The contemporary layman does not ordinarily meet this extreme position face-to-face; indeed, it is quite unlikely that he knows anyone who holds to this total contempt for the world view. But he does find himself surrounded by this view in many indirect ways. For example, the recently ordained priest mentioned at the beginning of this article, who could see human values only as instruments. And such a view is not confined to the newly ordained. The day after I received the letter I was discussing it with a pastor who told me, "I've been ordained for nineteen years and I've never thought of human values as anything but instruments."

There are dozens of other subtle ways in which the layman may meet this eschatological view. The emphasis on all things passing away, only eternity is important, what will all these material things mean a thousand years from now? The lack of interest he will find frequently in his fellow Catholics for the fine arts, for science, for the problem of freedom in the modern world—not that they don't accept these things, but merely that they take them for granted without seeing them in relation to the life of the spirit.

And yet despite all this, the layman cannot accept the idea that the world—in the sense of man and the whole of creation —is not worth it. He knows from personal experience that a great piece of music, an artistic masterpiece, a profound literary composition—all of these and many more elements of the world—stir him and make him more sensitive to the spiritual. He has the vivid example before him of Pope Pius XII on his deathbed, asking to listen to a Beethoven symphony. He feels that this is indeed grace building on nature. The fine things of the world are worthy objects in themselves and yield a certain human satisfaction. But insofar as they are good and true and beautiful he knows that they transcend the bounds of the natural and open his soul more readily to the supernatural.

Yet, if pressed hard enough, he is forced to admit it. In the long run only eternity counts. But this is not an either-or question. In terms of the historical process and of the end of history all things will pass away and only the Final Judgment stands as a reality against the backdrop of eternity. But in terms of *my* existence here in *my* city and state and nation in this year, these things are not passing away. They are both of this world and the next. And in view of what we know of the Second Coming and the Resurrection of the Body it is hard to accept the idea that all temporal values will be meaningless in eternity. The life of our soul is compounded of many things and it seems difficult to discard a lifetime of cultivation of human values, and goods, in eternity.

Thus, the layman, by virtue of his experience, and whether or not he recognizes the roots of the problem facing him, is driven irresistibly toward what Father Murray, in the same essay, calls incarnational humanism.

According to this view, "The end of man, it asserts, is indeed transcendent, supernatural; but it is an end of *man* and in its achievement man truly finds the perfection of his nature. Grace perfects nature, does not destroy it—this is the central point of emphasis. There is indeed a radical discontinuity between nature and grace, but nature does not therefore become irrelevant to grace. . . . Again, the perfect man of St. Paul will achieve the fullness of his age and stature only in heaven and not in history; nonetheless he grows in history. The Body of Christ is really a-building here in time. And its growth is that of a Body, not simply of a soul."

It seems to me that nothing short of incarnational humanism will adequately satisfy the spiritual and natural human needs of the educated American Catholic layman. Anything less will only stultify his humanity or his spirit.

Even in human terms, the sensitive Christian finds it difficult to regard people as instruments. For unless people are ends in themselves, it is all too easy to lose respect for human dignity, the eternal value of the individual human being. To tell a man involved in a Christian marriage with a woman and children he deeply loves that his wife and offspring are merely the means through which he is to work out his salvation may contain a textbook truth, but it goes contrary to the human intuition of all generations.

Perhaps, then, it is time to revise our terminology. God is in truth our ultimate end and all else is secondary—but secondary does not mean unimportant, nor does it necessarily connote the "instruments" idea. Traditionally, the primary end of marriage is the procreation and education of children; the secondary end is the mutual love and support and affection of the spouses. Humanly speaking, however, it is a rare couple who think in terms of anything but their mutual love when contemplating marriage. Their immediate goal is the secondary end and it is a worth-while one worthy of human dignity. Only in time will the ordinary couple see the fullness of the meaning of matrimony.

Similarly, men normally begin with the secondary ends that are most immediately apparent and comprehensible. Ultimately, they see the fullness of God's plan. They are not wasting their time with the good things of this earth. The only danger is that they be able to distinguish the secondary from the ultimate end and understand the proper relationship between the two.

"We have learned," writes Father Congar, "that though the work of the world is not the last end, neither is it *solely a means*; subordinate to the absolute end, it partakes of the character of means, but also of *intermediate end*, having its *own* value in its order. Accordingly it is appropriate that our commitment to it—in complete subordination to our supreme commitment to the faith—should be real and valid in its order too. We are engaged neither as to sheer means nor as to absolute end, but as to an intermediate end."

There is a further important consideration. If the things of this world—including the forms of government, the fine arts, and all human values—are only instruments, then what will really motivate the lay apostle to consider his work in this world of value and importance? Why not engage in what Father Murray calls basket-weaving? As he tells the story, "The old monk wove a basket one day; the next day he unwove it. The basket itself did not matter; but the weaving and unweaving of it served as a means of spending an interval, necessary to the frail human spirit, between periods of performance of the only task that did matter, the contemplation of heavenly things."

Indeed, why should lay apostles get all upset about conditions in the world? After all, the world will one day pass away. Instead of becoming involved in community organizations aimed at building a better society, why not spend the time to much better advantage making visits to our parish church? Certainly in view of what modern popes and bishops have taught about the role of the layman in the world today an answer is hardly needed—or is it?

If we pursue one view too far we end up neglecting the world; by pushing the other to its extreme we neglect the spirit. The only answer to solve the problem of human values for the layman is a carefully balanced approach which sees life in its true terms of immediate and eternal. But for such a view the idea of human values as mere shallow instruments will hardly do.

Pius XII put his finger on the crux of the matter in a 1951 address when he said:

"True religion and profound humaneness are not rivals. They are sisters. They have nothing to fear from one another, but everything to gain. Let each remain loyal to the law of its being, while it respects the vital needs and varied outward manifestations of the other, and the resultant harmonizing of two forces will endow any people engaged in the fulfillment of its appointed tasks with the most valuable incentives to real prosperity and solid progress."

CHAPTER 6

Spiritual Growth through Social Action

The problem of spirituality and spiritual growth is as old as man. It has been the subject of much of mankind's literature and for the religious man, at least, history itself is but a reflection of the eternal rise and fall of spirituality in the souls of men. What, then, can be said about spiritual formation and growth that hasn't already been said better before in a hundred different ways and as many languages? Probably nothing new. But . . . despite the awe-inspiring spiritual heritage of the Christian, the spiritual life is a new adventure, a unique experience for each new generation. Times change. So do societies and cultures. And so the old principles have to be polished up and applied anew to different situations.

In our own generation, we accentuate the layman and the social aspects of spirituality. In a highly complex, centralized, and interdependent type of society, social institutions sometimes take on a deadly and almost overwhelming importance and wield such an influence that man's spiritual life is profoundly influenced.

As a reaction to the evil found in so many of society's institutions, and aided and abetted by the spirit of individualism that has become so much a part of our American culture, many spiritually oriented persons withdraw from society. Repelled by the evil they see everywhere, they seek to avoid contact with it. This is no personal criticism of such persons—of whom observation indicates there are more than a few. Indeed, many of them become daily communicants and devote themselves to prayer and penance. Who is to judge them but the Divine Judge Himself?

But it is the thesis of this chapter that a more mature and

socially efficacious spiritual growth can take place in the average layman by *not* withdrawing from society. That closer union with Christ may be advanced in and through the very society which repels so many. That instead of withdrawing we must throw ourselves into the fray. It is possible for the layman to go through the world to God. Perhaps "possible" is too weak a word to use. A case might well be made that since the layman is in and of the world, he *must* in one way or another, proceed to God through the world.

Pope John speaks of this at length in *Mater et Magistra:* ". . . it would be an error if Our sons, especially the laity, should consider it more prudent to lessen their personal Christian commitment in the world. Rather should they renew and increase it.

"We should not," he says, "create an artificial opposition between the perfection of one's own being and one's personal active presence in the world, as if a man could not perfect himself except by putting aside all temporal activity and as if, however such action is done, a man is inevitably led to compromise his personal dignity as a human being and as a believer.

"Instead of this being so, it is perfectly in keeping with the plan of Divine Providence that each one develop and perfect himself through his daily work, which for almost all human beings is of a temporal nature."

How is the Church to make herself felt in the world? Pope John answers: ". . . the Church fulfills this mission through her lay sons, who should thus feel pledged to carry on their professional activities as the fulfillment of a duty, as the performance of a service in internal union with God and with Christ and for His glory."

In the world we see spiritual and physical evils which, because of our love for God, can become for us royal stepping-stones to sanctity as we practice the spiritual and corporal works of mercy or some other kind of action to alleviate these evils and attempt to make the spirit of Christ reign in ourselves, in others, and in the very warp and woof of society itself. Abbé Pierre must have this in mind as he continually preaches that through social action a person gets an awareness of God. It is possible, he implies, to touch God through feeding the hungry or working for social justice and social charity, just as we touch Him through contemplation.

Of course, the cycle is not complete, nor will our sanctity be complete, unless we return to contemplation. But the important point is that we must not neglect or underestimate the potential of spiritual growth open to us through action.

A word might be said here about the meaning of the terms action and social action. Both of them, as used here, refer primarily to external acts. That is, primarily actions which are aimed outside the individual—toward other individuals, groups, or even the social environment. The term social action is more appropriate when applied to action aimed at solving the "social question," which has occupied the minds of recent popes in their social encyclicals: i.e., social and economic life. It is not our purpose to attempt to define the words, so much as it is to distinguish them from interior action, such as individual meditation, saying the rosary, spiritual reading, etc.

Canon Cardijn gave a vivid example of the formative power of action in "Forming an Elite," an article in *New Life*:

"We must have faith in the worth of action to form and to transform.

"I have seen young fellows steeped in vice, the poor lads pretty well morbidly sexual. I have saved them all, everyone without exception by action. I would ask them to do this or that. After a time they would come along and tell me 'I don't seem to get time for that sort of thing now.' When they came back from the dance hall, their minds quite obsessed by their flirting with the girls there, I would give them a job to do. I would not stop to point out why they could not let themselves go on as they had been doing. I would bide my time, waiting for the psychological moment; straightway I gave them a job to do. There you have the formative power of action. Not words but acts! Simple acts, not a continuous stream of acts, just one here and there— 'Would you take this letter for me?'

'Would you have a word with a certain worker?' 'Would you say hello when you pass him in the street?' "

Social psychology affirms this approach in many interesting ways. Psychologists studying man's behavior in society have found that by setting up patterns of behavior it is possible to have an effect on the attitudes of the individuals following out these patterns.

A prejudiced person, for example, might well have his prejudices reduced considerably by being put into a situation in which he has to deal on an equal basis with members of minority groups. By being compelled to treat minorities as equals there is an almost inevitable subtle effect that is capable of gradually reforming a prejudiced individual's attitudes to the point where he begins to think of minorities as equals. Granting favorable circumstances, this is precisely what has happened to many men who have been forced to serve in the integrated armed forces.

Of course, it would be difficult to defend the thesis that a deep, living, interior spiritual growth flows unaided and *ex opere operato* from the performance of good acts alone. And I don't think that Canon Cardijn would hold that position. Yet, there is something to be said for the theory that an act can be the father of the thought. As Abbé Pierre indicates, the act can lead you back to God, although it does not necessarily have to do so.

Let's pursue this line of thought further. A group of priests in a Midwestern archdiocese has been exploring for some time the relation between social action and purity. It is their tentative conclusion that high school students who become involved in social movements, such as the Young Christian Students, are less likely to fall prey to impurity.

There is more involved here than merely keeping young people busy so that they don't have time for sin. The principle is that the entire emphasis and orientation of the Catholic social movements is directed outside the individual. Impurity is often found in persons who are inner-directed, who are selfish and concerned primarily with themselves. But the orientation of persons in the social movements is to be concerned for others and for the social and spiritual environment in which others live and work. By becoming involved in social action they forget self—with its connotation of impurity—and become concerned with others. For them, social action has spiritual values over and above the value of the action itself.

But this is not necessarily true for everyone engaged in such action. The director of adult education in a large archdiocese told this writer that he is continually perplexed by his experience that the graduates of secular universities are often more socially conscious than are the graduates of Catholic universities. This is reflected in the seemingly larger numbers of non-Catholics than Catholics engaged in community projects reflecting an interest in the field of social action: human relations work, social service centers, housing groups, etc. And yet not infrequently people engaged in such "religious" work profess no religion and they see no conflict between such activity and a man's personal morality. The protagonist of *Gentleman's Agreement*, for instance, is admired for his desire to eliminate anti-Semitism and the fact that his personal moral standards might approximate those of a tomcat does not distract from that admiration.

It seems a paradox to argue that social action is an excellent means of spiritual growth when, for many, conceivably most, of the people engaged in it spirituality is an alien subject. The resolution of the problem seems to lie with the individual rather than the action. True interior spiritual growth through social action can take place only in the spiritually oriented individual. But for such an individual it can become a path to sanctity.

What those who deprecate social action as a means of spiritual growth often forget is the nature of social action. They do not see that, upon analysis, social action is often really only the spiritual and corporal works of mercy extended into the facts of life in the twentieth century. Working for minimum wage legislation is certainly one way of helping to feed the hungry and clothe the naked. Striving for better housing is not unrelated to sheltering the homeless. And Catholic interracial, labor, and adult education groups are doing their share to instruct the ignorant.

An additional consideration concerns the modern lay movements that are constructed around the concept of spiritual growth through social action: Young Christian Students, Young Christian Workers, the Christian Family Movement, for example. All of them stress the importance of the social actions resulting from their social inquiries. The very structure of their meetings—with only fifteen minutes each set aside for the Gospel and the liturgy discussions, but forty-five minutes devoted to the social inquiry—reflect this orientation. Leaders of these movements are careful to point out that there is no dichotomy between the action taken as a result of the Gospel discussion and that flowing from the social inquiry. One is not spiritual and the other secular. On the contrary, both of them are regarded as "spiritual" in the sense that in the social inquiry an attempt is made to extend the spirit of the Gospels into some social situation, to Christianize a segment of social life.

For members of these apostolic groups, action is an expression of interior sentiments. But it is equally important to note that these exterior actions can and do help to bolster and reinforce the interior life of the individuals performing them. The repeated performance of good acts sets up a situation—an occasion of virtue, it might be called—in which the spiritual life might flourish all the more easily.

However, there are certain perils inherent in the concept of spiritual growth through social action that must not be overlooked. And the greatest danger, perhaps, is that the interior life might be sacrificed for the sake of devoting oneself to external actions. Being activists by nature, this is a fallacy into which Americans may easily fall. The only antidote is for us to comprehend that the measure of growth is in the individual soul and not in the type and extent of the actions performed. Within our frame of reference, a multiplication of successful actions means nothing unless it is accompanied by a concomitant deepened and enriched spirituality in the soul of the individual performing the actions.

In *Catholic Church, U.S.A.*, Father Jordan Aumann, O.P., makes this point when he writes in the chapter, *Activism and the Interior Life*, that "it is not what we do that makes us holy, but the charity that motivates us." Commenting on activism, he observes that "the ideal to be proposed is that the apostolate and all good works should proceed from a profound interior life. And while it is true that a spiritual formation is possible through action, the external good works receive their value and merit from the charity that impels them and are themselves dispositions to contemplation and the exercises of the interior life. It is only in this restricted sense that we can subscribe to the doctrine of a spirituality of action. But to make the external works or even the apostolate an end in themselves is to fall victim to what Pope Pius XII has called 'the heresy of action.'"

However, the coin has two sides. It is too easy to delay participation in essential social action on the grounds that we have not yet completed our forty days in the desert, that we need more preparation before undertaking the active life. There is always the danger that we may falsely identify our interior life as "spiritual" and the exterior life as "secular," when, in actuality, our exterior life must be an extension of our inner spirituality into the world. We must never lose sight of the fact that our social actions can also be spiritual actions which will contribute to our spiritual formation, to the strengthening of our interior spirituality.

The fount of life for the priest, religious, or layman engaged in social action is to be found in contemplation and the liturgy, but because these essential acts are vivifying they impel the social actionist to further action and greater efforts. And authentic Christian social action in itself works subtly and often imperceptibly to lead the social actionist closer to the Source of his action. Interior life and social action thus blend into one continuous act of love and self-giving, which reflect an intimate sharing of divine life. That is the real meaning of spiritual growth through social action.

CHAPTER 7

The Liturgy and the Lay Apostolate

It is no accident that the growth of the liturgical movement and the lay apostolate have taken place at the same time in modern American history. It is, I believe, strictly providential. Twenty years ago the average layman had no idea but the vaguest about either movement; today, they are both discussed so much in some circles they are in danger of losing some of their effect by reason of repetition. Yet, you simply cannot discuss one without the other, for they must be as intimately related in practice as they are in theory if either is to be fully successful.

As far back as 1929, the American liturgical pioneer, Dom Virgil Michel, as related in *Virgil Michel and the Liturgical Movement*, spoke of "the inseparability of the liturgical life and Catholic Action. . . . Catholic Action is but the further development of the liturgical life. . . . Not only are the liturgical life and Catholic Action inseparable, but the two go to the very heart of the Christian dispensation. . . .

"The true significance of the liturgical movement, therefore, lies just in this: that it tries to lead men back to the 'primary and indispensable source of the true Christian spirit'; it tries to restore that of which Catholic Action is the further flowering and fruitage."

Unfortunately, despite all the publicity and the public discussion, the meaning of the liturgy and the liturgical movement is still no more clear to the average American Catholic than is the lay apostolate—perhaps even less so. The reason for this situation is certainly not because the idea of the liturgy is complicated. Actually the liturgy is relatively simple to define. Basically, it comprises the Mass and the sacraments, plus the Divine Office, which the priest says in his breviary every day. In his famous encyclical on the liturgy, *Mediator Dei*, Pope Pius XII gave his own formal definition: "The sacred liturgy is consequently the public worship which our Redeemer as Head of the Church renders to the Father as well as the worship which the community of the faithful renders to its Founder, and through Him to the Heavenly Father. It is, in short, the worship offered by the Mystical Body of Christ in the entirety of its Head and members." And he adds, later on, ". . . the most pressing duty of Christians is to live the liturgical life, and increase and cherish its supernatural spirit."

It is all very neat and short and simple: The liturgy and the lay apostolate are as inseparable as man and wife. They depend on each other; they complement one another. It has been said regularly since 1926—the date when the Benedictine Fathers' Liturgical Press in Collegeville, Minnesota, was founded and Father Virgil Michel began editing *Orate Fratres* (now *Worship*), the pioneer magazine of the American liturgical movement.

If we want to count noses, it is safe to say that never before in the history of the Church in America have so many laymen attended Mass so often and received Holy Communion so frequently. Many measures have been taken in recent years to make it more and more easy to participate in the liturgy. The Eucharistic fast laws have been relaxed. The famous "September [1958] Instruction" on sacred music and the liturgy by the Sacred Congregation of Rites encouraged increased participation in the liturgy by the laity. The Holy Week liturgy has been restored, making the celebration of that week a memorable religious experience for all who take part.

Although, unfortunately, in some places there has not been any great enthusiasm for these changes, they have been received wholeheartedly in many dioceses, where they have resulted in greatly renewed liturgical life in countless parishes. And it is probably true to say that more lay people in the United States know more about the meaning of the liturgy than ever before.

Yet, there is something missing. Despite the valiant work of the priests and lay people of the liturgical movement all these years, even today when their annual conventions are overflow affairs, still something is lacking. We cannot honestly say today that all or most or even the majority of American Catholic laymen understand what the liturgy is really all about, that it is a vital force in their daily lives.

I do not say this in criticism of the liturgical movement, for its leaders are well aware of the task that remains before them. And especially since 1960, when they organized a national office with a full-time layman as executive secretary, they have made remarkable, systematic progress.

But neither the liturgical movement nor the lay apostolate will flourish in the United States until they can overcome the basic difficulty which confronts them both. The core of this problem is that for most American Catholics religion is a private, personal affair. Their devotional life has been built for so many years around what has been called the "Jesus and I" concept that all this talk about the liturgy goes over their heads. For them the Mass is primarily and simply a personal religious experience. They go, sometimes even daily, to Mass and Communion because of what it can do for them. Their prayers are almost always prayers of petition.

I do not mean to ridicule these people, for they are more often than not really good people personally, and most of them have never been taught any differently. Further, they are only following the traditional American code that religion is an individual matter. If you allow it to intrude too much into your conversation or deeds, you are likely to be labeled a "Holy Joe."

So, I mean only to describe these people when I say they are usually the ones who oppose the introduction of the dialogue Mass or congregational singing at Mass. Their reason is simply that such modern goings-on distracts them from their private prayers. They have grown up with the idea that the Mass is something the priest says quietly and efficiently at the altar while they go about their own business and say their own prayers. They simply do not understand the social implications of the Mass and the sacraments.

And the Mass can be a profound religious experience for these people. Slipping into the back pew of a cool, almost deserted church for a 7 A.M. Mass at the beginning of a hot summer day . . . or attending the same Mass during the winter months when the rest of the world is asleep and it is still dark outside—it can make you feel close to God, separated from the cares and woes of this vale of tears for a brief half-hour.

No doubt about it, it's expecting a lot to think that a person reared in this tradition will eagerly switch to a 5:30 P.M. dialogue or sung Mass crowded with mothers and fathers and children wandering in and out of pews, distracted from personal communion with God by the singing or by the responses of the congregation to the priest's salutations.

Yet, because it seems quite clear that the Church wants the celebration of Mass to be in a manner which gives the greatest opportunity to join in offering the Holy Sacrifice and at a time convenient for the most people, we must, I think, at least ask ourselves why the Church takes this attitude?

The doctrine that the Church is the Mystical Body of Christ on earth and that in this Body we are united to Christ and to each other and to every other member throughout time and in the world is an essential part of the reason why. The Mass is *not* just a private affair between the priest and the congregation. It involves the whole Mystical Body in whose name and for whom it is offered. The Mass is the sacrament of unity, not of isolation. It is also an opportunity for instruction and to offer publicly to the Eternal Father the worship we owe Him with our hearts, our minds, our souls—indeed, even with our voices. It is virtually impossible to partake fully in the offering of the Holy Sacrifice if we isolate ourselves in the last pew of the church, shutting out the world around us so we can concentrate on our rosary.

It is, therefore, precisely because the Mass is a great social act that we should not and cannot allow ourselves to become "mute spectators," withdrawn from the celebrant, from our fellow members of the congregation, and from our fellow members of the Mystical Body. There is a time and a need for meditation, but normally the Mass is not that time.

I mentioned above that the quiet Mass in the quiet church with a quiet congregation can have the great psychological effect on us of withdrawing us from the world. Perhaps this explains all too well why the liturgy is not a dynamic, driving force in the lives of American Catholics and the society in which they live. Too many quiet Masses in quiet churches with quiet congregations has led us to look upon the Mass as a personal encounter with Christ by which we can separate ourselves from the world. We have come to look upon the Mass as an end in itself with great personal consolations—and few people have told us better.

Do not misunderstand. I am not saying that the Mass is not an end or an act complete in itself. It is obvious that the public worship of God in the Holy Sacrifice stands by itself; it is not merely a means to an end. But neither is it only an end. It is much more besides. Its purpose is unity—the opposite of isolation. Its purpose is not only to unite us to God but to the world and to our fellow members of the Mystical Body as well. Its purpose is to form and inspire us as members of the lay apostolate.

The Mass becomes a mockery if we devoutly assist at the altar and then step outside the church door and discriminate, violate social justice and charity, fail to work for the christianization of society, or generally neglect the work of the apostolate in our own environment.

In *The Dynamics of Liturgy*, a pioneer in the movement, both in Germany and the United States, Father H. A. Reinhold says: "Justice and charity cannot be excluded: the liturgy carried out to perfection, not only exteriorly, but even with the knowledge and spiritual disposition striven after by the best liturgists, will be a tinkling cymbal in the ears of God unless the ones who celebrate it continue to glorify the same Lord in the economic, social, political, and cultural fields."

To be guilty of separating the sacred liturgy from our daily life is to pervert our vocation as Christians, as brothers of Christ and His brothers in the Mystical Body. What I believe is a classic example of what happens when the liturgy is relegated to the sanctuary was told me by a Southern priest when I was visiting a Deep South city with a large Catholic population.

"Our problem here," he said, "is not the fallen-aways or the anti-Catholic bigots. Our problem is the good Catholic, the daily communicant who doesn't understand what being a Catholic really means." He went on, then, to explain that the leaders of the segregation movement among the Catholics in his city were almost all daily participants in the Eucharistic Banquet. He did not attempt to judge their motives or consciences; for he felt they were ill-instructed. But his story did point up clearly the necessity of seeing the Mass whole, not just as something we go to, but as something we live.

When near the end of the Mass the priest turns and says, "*Ite, missa est,*" he is not really saying, "Go, the Mass is ended." His real meaning is: "Go, your soul has been fortified with the Body and Blood of Christ, your mind has been informed and you have been inspired by this contact with your Redeemer. Now, go out into your parish, your business, your community, your world and act as a Christian. Put into practice the lessons of the Mass. Be Christ to the world. And then come back again bringing your life from the end of this Mass to the beginning of the next to offer to Christ. Go, but remember that for the real Christian the Mass never ends."

The Mass, then, is something real and living. It has a basic role to play in politics, interracial justice, the family, and international life. The meaning of the Mass in our own daily lives and how it should affect our society was the subject of a convention of the liturgical movement some years ago. By studying some of the things which were said at this significant meeting, we might be able to see more clearly that the relationship between the Mass and the world in which we live is a real one.

Take, for example, the race problem, which is always so much on our minds these days.

Speaking of the race question and the Mass, Bishop Vincent S. Waters of Raleigh, North Carolina, told the liturgical conference that "the Mass is the greatest union because it is a union of action with Christ. We, although we are and remain individuals, become one in our common action, in offering the Mass with Christ. If we are with Christ, we are with each other.

"The Mass means, makes, presupposes union. 'First, go reconcile thyself with thy brother and then go offer thy gift.'

"The Mass alone," he added, "like the Redemption, can bring about complete interracial justice."

In political life, the Mass has a living role to play also. It is, of course, no substitute for good politicians or a vigorous political life with plenty of citizen participation. But, as Msgr. George Higgins, director of the Social Action Department of the National Catholic Welfare Conference pointed out, the Mass is "the primary source of asceticism and penance without which there can be no conversion from human selfishness or sin and no redemption of individuals or the temporal order."

Despite all the talk about internationalism, few indeed are the Catholics who would connect the Mass with international life. Yet, this is the subject of one of the major addresses at the liturgical convention to which we have been referring.

Bishop John J. Wright, now Bishop of Pittsburgh, declared that one of the primary questions we must ask ourselves is "How far does my Mass make me one with Jesus Christ? For He, the Priest and Victim of our Mass, is the Son of Man, not of any one nation alone; the hero of all our race, not of any one people alone; . . . our Redeemer for eternity; our teacher, and our hope in realizing personal peace or the international order for which the clear of head and the clean of heart so ardently pray."

Speaking of the reigning pontiff at that time, Pope Pius XII, Bishop Wright said: "No living voice speaking on the lofty levels of international leadership has more consistently argued for the need of an organized international community than has that of the Holy Father. . . .

"The Holy Father has sometimes clearly offended the ultra-nationalistic and isolationist sentiments of many of his own people, not only in this country, but wherever else the sensitive spirit of undisciplined nationalism dies hard. He is confident, no doubt, that in the final issue all superficial commitments of a narrowly partisan character will yield to the higher and more universal loyalties of those in every land who share the solidarity of one Lord, one Faith and one Baptism; who are made one Body because nourished by one Bread; who, at their several altars, are quickened by the life-giving energies of one sacrifice, the Holy Sacrifice of the Mass."

Developing his point further, Bishop Wright said also that "the pronouncements of the Holy Father concerning the special responsibility of Catholics towards the achievement of an international community and his pronouncements concerning the place of the Mass in the lives of individuals and nations" are really two sides of the same problem.

Discussing the relationship of the Mass to family unity, Bishop John R. MacDonald of Antigonish, Nova Scotia, asked, "How can there be any lasting dissension in a family or among families, the members of which are active participants at Holy Mass and frequent communicants?"

Bishop MacDonald made clear one of the most significant points we must remember about the relationship of the Mass to the apostolate when he declared that the apostolate for Catholic families is to save family life from our modern secularistic environment.

"This apostolate," he said, "is spiritual in its foundation, as well as in its motives and in its most powerful means. But it is not solely spiritual. Family life is sick. Where there is sickness, one does more than pray. There are social and economic causes, as well as basic spiritual deficiencies. The family apostolate cannot neglect any of these. Social and economic obstacles to Christian family living must be removed."

To the layman who has never thought much about the

liturgy before, these concepts are thrilling, opening up to him a whole new facet of his religious life. They make the Mass and the entire liturgy more meaningful; a lot of things begin to fall into place; the pieces begin to fit together and from many scattered fragments of religious knowledge a unified picture begins to emerge. There is no division between our worship and our daily life; they are so intimately related that true worship will extend itself into every aspect of our life. If he knows what the liturgy is all about, the man of prayer is forced to become a man of action—and the man of action must return to prayer, especially that public prayer of the Church which is the liturgy, in order to provide himself with the spiritual tools for his life of action.

Dom Virgil Michel, writing in *Orate Fratres*, put it into a frequently quoted syllogism: "Pius X tells us that the liturgy is the indispensable source of the true Christian spirit; Pius XI says that the true Christian spirit is indispensable for social regeneration. Hence the conclusion: The liturgy is the indispensable basis of Christian social regeneration."

The liturgist must become a social actionist and the social actionist a liturgist. The liturgical movement, the lay apostolate, the social action movement, are not really separate movements, except to secure immediate results in their own special fields. Actually, they are all only parts of the broader picture—the multifaceted vocation of the Christian. In the world today, the normal life of the layman requires that he be all three—a liturgist, a social actionist, a lay apostle. Circumstances may require that an individual layman devote most of his time to one or the other of these facets of the Christian life, but never to the total exclusion of the others.

To keep our perspectives clear, however, let us never forget that the liturgy must be at the hub of our prayer life and our apostolate. It is the "indispensable source" around which we must organize our lives; but never let us be content with a more full and deeper participation in the Mass alone. Christ invites and urges us to come to Him in the Mass and the Eucharist. But the same Christ in His own words and the words of His vicars in their social encyclicals insists that from the wellsprings of the Mass we draw the inspiration and divine grace we need to continue the work of the liturgy in the world.

Virgil Michel summarized the dynamic relationship between the liturgy and the lay apostolate in a memorable passage, which should be emblazoned on the first page of every book on the lay apostolate:

"Is there any wonder that the life of so many Christians is made up of a minimum of passive submission to rules and formulas in matters religious, and a maximum of activities outside the church in matters secular? In other words, the Christian becomes active in life in proportion as he is removed from the altar, which is just the opposite of what should be taking place, of what is demanded by the true Christian spirit. If we seek for an answer to the question of why Christians have functioned so little as lay apostles in the world in our centuries, we have it here. The entire life of the true Christian . . . must be a reflection and a further expression of his life at the altar of God, at the true source of the Christian spirit. If he is predominantly a passive Christian there, can we expect him to be an active Christian in his daily life out in the world?"

This is why we must make every effort to implement the wish of the Popes that the liturgy become in every parish the vital center of parochial life. For it is the liturgy which will vivify and give meaning to all our activities in the world. And, as Virgil Michel notes so well, unless we take part in the liturgy we shall not take part in the apostolate.

The truth of this is easily confirmed. Study the Church in America. Where is the lay apostolate most active, most dynamic? Check each archdiocese, each diocese, each parish. Is the liturgy there an actuality? Is it preached in its entirety and practiced by the priest and the people? There is where you will find the lay apostolate at its best. There is where you will find responsible and mature laymen.

I have been asked many times about a particular large archdiocese in the United States. "Why," the question goes, "does the lay apostolate flourish so in this archdiocese? Why have laymen been able to accomplish so much? Why do laymen play such a leading and important role in the life of the Church there and even throughout the nation?"

The answer, I believe, is simply because the lay apostolate and the liturgical movement in that archdiocese have grown hand in hand. Of all the lay and clerical leaders there involved in the work of the lay apostolate or in specific social action work, I know none who is not also an ardent liturgist, active in promoting the liturgy. They have seen through the years of their work the need of that "indispensable source" to give them stability, inspiration and Christian maturity. They have learned that from the liturgy they can get the divine life and grace they need to go about their Father's business in the world. They have learned also that their work means nothing unless they can take it to the altar and offer it back to the Source of all things.

And I have found this to be true likewise of other dioceses and of particular parishes within an archdiocese or diocese. It is almost axiomatic that where the liturgical movement in its fullness is preached, or at least understood, there you will find a healthy lay movement and a dynamic social action movement. Contrariwise, in those places in the United States where the liturgical movement is frowned upon or not encouraged, you will almost always find a weak lay movement or that the concept of the lay apostolate is confined to the idea of the layman being a kind of assistant to the priest.

Our past and present experience shows clearly that we have our work cut out for us. Christ will not be brought by laymen into the world of today until He is first brought to those laymen through the liturgy of the Church. The future of both the lay apostolate and the liturgical movement depends on how well they can learn to work together to solve their mutual problems.

CHAPTER 8

Tools for the Layman

The success of the lay apostolate in the United States (or any other place, for that matter) is going to depend on two major factors: spiritual formation and an effective grasp of the Church's social teachings.

Everyone connected with the lay apostolate sees immediately the necessity of a deep spiritual formation for the apostle, including both personal spiritual development and at least a working knowledge of simple theology. Unfortunately, not everyone understands the equally vital need for laymen to have a firm grounding in the social doctrine of the Church—though why they don't is certainly puzzling.

Perhaps the reason for this is because many of the people who have been charged with the work of the lay apostolate do not themselves understand or know enough about these social teachings and their value as indispensable tools for the layman in the construction of a Christian society. There seems no other way to explain it. For it is inconceivable that anyone who had done even a superficial reading of the Church's major social documents should not note the insistent pleading of pope after pope in our times for a more widespread and incisive teaching of Christian social principles as the basis for the solution of the major social, economic, and political problems (including communism) of the modern world.

Certainly it was never stated more strongly than by Pope John XXIII in *Mater et Magistra* when he said: "We reaffirm strongly that the Christian social doctrine is an integral part of the Christian conception of life."

He added that it is indispensable "that this doctrine be known, assimilated and translated into social reality in the form and manner that the different situations allow and demand. It is a most difficult task, but a most noble one, to the carrying out of which We must warmly invite not only Our brothers and sons scattered throughout the world but also all men of good will."

Not satisfied with this general appeal, Pope John became even more specific and pointed out that Catholic social teaching must "be extended by regular systematic courses in Catholic schools of every kind, especially in seminaries. It is to be inserted into the religious instruction programs of parishes and of associations of the lay apostolate. It should be spread by every association of the lay apostolate. It should be spread by every modern means of expression—daily newspapers and periodicals, publications of both a scientific and popular nature, radio and television."

And he added: ". . . it is not enough for this education that men be taught their social obligations. They must also be given by practical action the methods that will enable them to fulfill their duties."

How can we explain the preoccupation of modern popes with the social doctrine of the Church? It is simply and directly because this doctrine is the major source from which we get the information we need about what kind of a society the Church wants us to construct and what principles we must follow to accomplish that end. Christian social principles lay down the ground rules we must follow to build a Christian and human world; they provide us with the tools we need if society is ever to become Christian again.

Our purpose here is to examine some of these tools we shall need to be effective lay apostles, but first it is in order to take up some basic, prior questions— Why does the Church speak on social matters? With what authority? How does she speak to us?

I suppose it should not be surprising that there are still some Catholics who find it difficult to accept the Church's right to speak or who scoff at papal statements when they are issued. After all, in 1931 in commemorating the fortieth anniversary of Leo XIII's *On the Condition of Labor*, Pope Pius XI noted "that the teaching of Leo XIII, so noble and lofty and so utterly new to worldly ears, was held suspect by some, even among Catholics, and to certain ones it gave grave offense."

Nonetheless, the reasons why Pope Leo XIII had the right to speak in 1891 were the same ones which authorized Pope John XXIII to issue *Mater et Magistra* in 1961. And chief among these reasons is the intimate relationship between social conditions and spirituality.

Our souls are not disembodied spirits above time and clime. The state of our physical health, the condition of social health of the society in which we live—both play a significant part in our spiritual lives, for weal or woe. We simply cannot discuss spirituality without taking into account the physical and social conditions in which this spirituality exists.

The American bishops made this point in their 1940 statement on *The Church and the Social Order* when they said: "Who can deny the close relationship between economic injustice and a long train of evils, physical, social and moral? Unfair wages . . . due to false and immoral economic principles lead directly to undernourishment, bad housing, inadequate clothing and indirectly to irregular family relations, child delinquency and crime. . . . Because human beings and not animated machines toil in industry, therefore the Church cannot abdicate her right and duty to speak out in defense of the rights of human personality nor fail to declare uncompromisingly the moral obligations of industrial and economic life."

As the American bishops point out, their right to speak also imposes a duty to do so. They are not free to speak or not to speak on social, economic, and political matters that seriously affect the spiritual lives of the souls under their care; they *must* speak out in such cases.

Pope Pius XI made this quite clear in his 1931 encyclical *On Reconstructing the Social Order:*

". . . there resides in Us the right and duty to pronounce with supreme authority upon social and economic matters.

Certainly the Church was not given the commission to guide men to an only fleeting and perishable happiness but to that which is eternal. Indeed 'the Church holds that it is unlawful for her to mix without cause in these temporal concerns'; however, she can in no wise renounce the duty God entrusted to her to interpose her authority, not of course in matters of technique for which she is neither suitably equipped nor endowed by office, but in all things that are connected with the moral law. For as to these, the deposit of truth that God committed to Us and the grave duty of disseminating and interpreting the whole moral law, and of urging it in season and out of season, bring under and subject to Our supreme jurisdiction not only social order but economic activities themselves."

Every human act, ethics tells us, has a moral aspect. This includes our acts in political, economic, and social life as well as those of a purely religious nature. In other words, all man's acts must conform both to his nature and to Revelation. It is particularly with these moral aspects of our acts, alone or in society, that the Church is concerned. She does not presume to intervene in technical matters, as Pope Pius notes. For example, she does not say that a democracy is a better form of government than a constitutional monarchy, but she does insist that every form of government must respect the basic rights of its citizens. She does not tell a manufacturer how to merchandise his product, but she does say that he may not misrepresent it. She does not declare that you must support every union demand, but she does require that you respect the right of men to organize into unions.

Assuming the right and duty of the Church to speak on the moral aspects of man's life in society, the question still remains as to the authority of such pronouncements. It is not possible to give a simple black-and-white catechism answer to this question, but there are certain clear-cut principles to be followed.

For instance, there is the famous passage in Pope Pius XII's encyclical *Humani Generis*, which takes up this matter specifically:

"Nor must it be thought that what is expounded in encyclical letters does not of itself demand consent, since in writing such letters the Popes do not exercise the supreme power of their teaching authority. For these matters are taught with the ordinary teaching authority, of which it is true to say: 'He who heareth you, heareth me'; and generally what is expounded and inculcated in encyclical letters already for other reasons appertains to Catholic doctrine. But if the Supreme Pontiffs in their official documents purposely pass judgment on a matter up to that time under dispute, it is obvious that that matter, according to the mind and will of the same Pontiffs, cannot be any longer considered a question open to discussion among theologians."

Earlier in his Pentecost message in 1941, Pius XII had put it this way (italics added):

"Do not let die in your midst and fade away the insistent call of the *social encyclicals*, that voice which indicated to the faithful in the supernatural regeneration of mankind the *moral obligation* to cooperate in the arrangement of society, and especially of economic life, exhorting those who share in this life to action no less than the State itself. Is this not a *sacred duty* for every Christian?"

An authority on the encyclicals, the late Bishop Francis J. Haas commented once that "the Popes have issued the encyclicals not as mere expressions of opinion which Catholics may either accept or ignore, but rather as doctrinal pronouncements which place Catholics under the obligation of yielding to these pronouncements the obedience of mind and will."

And Bishop William T. Mulloy of Covington, Kentucky, stated: "It is due time that Catholics come to realize that they cannot excuse themselves from grave sin if they deliberately disregard or deride the contents of the social papal encyclicals. . . ."

Commenting in *The Voice of St. Jude* on "the binding force of teaching contained in radio addresses and public addresses" (by the Pope), Bishop John J. Wright of Pittsburgh stated: "The answer to the question: 'Do these talks impose on Catholics the obligation to accept the statements made in them or are Catholics free to reject statements which are at variance with their own opinion?' is: These statements are to be accepted with religious assent." And "religious assent," he explained, "is a true internal assent. Its motive is not the authority of God speaking, nor is it precisely the infallibility of the Church's teaching authority, but rather the official position of the Supreme Teacher. The certitude in 'religious assent' can perhaps be compared to *practical* certitude, the certitude we use so much in daily living. For example, reason cannot exclude all danger of accident every time we board a bus, a train or a plane. Yet the danger of accident is sufficiently excluded to warrant a prudent man's traveling."

The question remains: *How* does the Church speak to us?

From the standpoint of authority, the two greatest sources of teaching about man in society are the pope and the bishops. We have, earlier, cited the American bishops' statement of 1940; they have made many others of special social significance, including their notable message of 1958 on racial discrimination. The bishops of most other countries also issue periodic messages on social affairs, often applying social principles to special conditions within their own areas of jurisdiction.

Perhaps the most systematic exposition of Catholic social teaching, however, is to be found in the encyclicals, addresses, and allocutions of the popes since the reign of Leo XIII. Six of these encyclicals stand out for their clear and authoritative presentation of Christian social principles or related matters.

Four of these are social encyclicals: Leo XIII's *Rerum Novarum* (*On the Condition of Labor*) issued in 1891; Pius XI's two great encyclicals, *Quadragesimo Anno* (*On the Reconstruction of the Social Order*) in 1931 and *Divini Redemptoris* (*On Atheistic Communism*) in 1937; and most recently Pope John's *Mater et Magistra* (*Mother and Teacher*, also called *Christianity and Social Progress*) in 1961, the longest and most complete of the social encyclicals running to some 25,-000 words.

Pius XII of all modern popes has been the most prolific in terms of the vast amount of his pronouncements on social, economic, and political matters. But in terms of social relationships, he probably will be most remembered for two encyclicals on "social spirituality"—*Mystici Corporis Christi* (*The Mystical Body of Christ*) in 1943 and *Mediator Dei* (*The Sacred Liturgy*) in 1947. These two priceless documents provide the theological and liturgical basis for the lay apostolate and the social doctrine of the Church. They are concerned with the social aspects of man's spirituality and are indispensable for any broad understanding of the Church's teaching.

Papal encyclicals are relatively modern in the history of the Church. They date back to Benedict XIV, who issued one in December, 1740, on the duties of bishops; since Gregory XVI (1831–46), they have been used more and more by the popes. The word encyclical itself means circular letter, or letter to be circulated. Most of them are addressed by the pope to the bishops who are supposed to pass them on to their people; exceptions to this are Pius XI's *On the Reconstruction of the Social Order* and John XXIII's *Mother and Teacher*, which were addressed directly to the faithful as well as the hierarchy.

Encyclicals aren't restricted to social doctrine. Generally, however, they are of two kinds: Those which deal with dogmatic or religious subjects such as those on the Mystical Body, the rosary, retreats, and marriage, or the social encyclicals, which are concerned primarily with social, economic, and political matters.

It should be noted too that the basic social encyclicals speak usually in terms of broad, general natural law principles. The Church does not attempt to lay down a detailed and specific blueprint for the reconstruction of society. Rather she establishes principles and ground rules which should guide us and which allow considerable variation in specific application from place to place; since encyclicals are directed to the

Church throughout the world this is certainly necessary, for it would be difficult to be specific about the application of principles to countries ranging from the most modern civilization of the Western world to the most underdeveloped emerging nation in Africa or Asia.

This does not mean the Church is so vague as to be meaningless; it does mean, however, that there is significant room for differences in application of specific principles. It is easy to trace the effect, for instance, that changing times have had on the emphasis given by individual popes to certain teachings. Take the matter of the role of the state. Both Leo XIII in 1891 and Pius XI in 1931 stressed the right of the state to intervene in economic matters. But Leo XIII was writing at a time in history when economic liberalism was in full flower and many people denied the right of the state to intervene in the economy even to protect exploited workers, so he took a strong position in favor of the state's right to protect the poor and oppressed. Forty years later, Pius XI did not minimize this right. But in 1931 he could look out of his Vatican window and see a totalitarian state in his front yard, so he stressed also that it was important for the state to maintain a respect for individual liberty. And he pointed out the need for intermediary groups to exist between the state and the individual to protect the individual from the power of the omnipotent state.

Both Leo and Pius accepted the same teaching, but because of historical circumstances they emphasized different aspects of it.

The first consideration, even in a cursory examination of some of the church's major social teachings must be the dignity of the individual, for this concept is at the very heart of all Catholic social teaching. As Pope John notes in *Mater et Magistra:* "The fundamental principle [of Catholic social doctrine] . . . is . . . that individual human beings are and should be the foundation, the end and the subjects of all the institutions in which social life is carried on, that is, individual human souls considered insofar as they are and should be by their nature intrinsically social, and insofar as they are in the plan of Providence, and by their elevation to the supernatural order."

The individual is the center of Catholic social thought because the Church has a vital concern for the soul of every individual human being. God wants the freely given love of free men and every society must strive to make it possible for men to be as free as they can to choose the will of Christ. This concern was expressed by Pius XII in his Christmas Message of 1942:

"The origin and the primary scope of social life is the conservation, development, and perfection of the human person, helping him to realize accurately the demands and values of religion and culture set by the Creator for every man and for all mankind. . . . A social teaching or a social reconstruction program which denies or prescinds from this internal essential relation to God of everything that regards man, is on a false course; and while it builds up with the one hand, it prepares with the other the materials which sooner or later will undermine and destroy the whole fabric."

It must be understood that this is not a theory of unrestrained individualism, for to balance the "individualism" expressed in the papal documents is the concept of the common good. This corresponds roughly to our Founding Fathers' idea of the general welfare and it is generally a condition in which both the goods of individuals and the good of society as a whole are reconciled. In other words, the rights of individuals make sense only within the framework of the good of the entire society.

In working for a better society, the layman is often faced with the problem of the role of the state. Again, here, Catholic social doctrine provides him with the tools he needs to work surely and in a Christian and human manner for the construction of a decent society.

It is the state which is the protector and promoter of the common good in Catholic social thought. As Pope John explains in *Mater et Magistra*:

"The state, the reason for whose existence is the realization of the common good in the temporal order, cannot keep aloof from the economic world. It should be present to promote in a suitable manner the production of a sufficient supply of material goods, 'the use of which is necessary for the practice of virtue,' and to watch over the rights of all citizens, especially of the weaker, such as workers, women and children. It is also its ineluctable task to contribute actively to the betterment of the condition of life of the workers.

"It is further the duty of the state to see to it that work regulations are regulated according to justice and equity and that in the environment of work the dignity of the human spirit is not violated in body or spirit."

But just as the concept of the common good prevents individualism from getting out of hand, so does the principle of subsidiarity prevent the state from interfering unduly in the life of men. The tool of the principle of subsidiarity is a handy and necessary one for the layman who is trying to strike a delicate balance between the right of the state on the one hand to work for men and on the other hand the danger that the state will intervene too often so as to interfere with man's freedom. It was Pope Pius XI in *On Reconstructing the Social Order* who gave the classic definition of subsidiarity:

"This is a fundamental principle of social philosophy, unshaken and unchangeable. Just as it is wrong to withdraw from the individual and commit to the community at large what private enterprise and industry can accomplish, so too is it an injustice, a grave evil and a disturbance of right order for a larger and higher organization to arrogate to itself functions which can be performed efficiently by smaller and lower bodies; of its very nature, the true aim of all social activity should be to help individual members of the social body, but never to destroy or absorb them."

The tool of subsidiarity gives the layman a handy guide to prevent him from falling into ultraconservativism, which denies the right of the state to intervene at all, and ultraliberalism, which tends to rely too promiscuously on the state's assistance in solving social problems.

The basic tool that the layman must have, however, if he is going to be effective in the temporal order, is a grasp of the fundamental social teaching of the Church that the reconstruction of society is going to be brought about only by a twofold approach—the reform of morals and the reform of institutions. So often we feel unsure of how we can approach this giant task we have of making society Christian. It is not an easy answer, but nonetheless the answer is that we have to change both individuals and the social institutions which influence them. And to bring this about we must practice two social virtues—social justice and social charity.

In general, justice is described as the virtue which constantly disposes the will to give to everyone what is his due. There is commutative justice, which involves a relationship of rights and duties between two or more persons. Thus, an employee would be bound by commutative justice to give a full day's work for a day's pay. There is also distributive justice, which is concerned with the obligations of the community to distribute its burdens and benefits fairly: The rich are required to pay more tax proportionately than the poor.

In addition, there is social justice, which is the obligation upon individuals to participate, according to their ability and position, in *group action*, designed to make the *institutions of society* conform to the *common good* in the temporal order.

In the words of Pope Pius XI in *On Atheistic Communism:* "In reality, besides commutative justice, there is also social justice with its own set obligations from which neither employers nor workingmen can escape. Now it is of the very essence of social justice to demand from each individual all that is necessary for the common good."

Another idea spelled out by the popes—particularly Pius XI —is that of reorganizing economic life into what has been called in the United States the Industry Council Plan. The idea is for business and labor to cooperate, with public representatives, for the economic common good of the nation and the world. The core principle is that economic life should be organized to seek the common good rather than the economic advantage of any single segment of society.

This helps explain why the Church has always been so concerned about workers and employers organizing into unions and employers' associations. For unless they are organized they cannot cooperate together effectively. Of course, an additional reason is because responsible unions and employers' groups can help safeguard the rights and dignity of the individual, who is the major concern of our social doctrine.

Applying the need for social organization to the world community has been the particular work of Pius XII and John XXIII. Pope Pius especially worked out in some detail a set of teachings through his various addresses and writings on international life. And in *Mater et Magistra* Pope John also spells out the obligations of Catholics in the international community particularly in regard to foreign aid.

These are only a few of the basic social teachings of the Church, which are indispensable tools for laymen who hope to build the kind of society called for repeatedly by modern pontiffs. To get the total picture it is essential that every layman read and study all the papal social documents. Admittedly, this is not easy work, but then the popes have never said that being an effective lay apostle is easy—but it is necessary lest the world be lost to the forces of evil. Whether Christianity is to play a major role in the society of the future will depend in large part on how well laymen learn to use the tools of Catholic social doctrine. The success of the lay apostolate is going to depend not only on holy laymen, but equally on laymen who know and understand the Church's social teachings.

CHAPTER 9

Using the Tools

A great paradox of our times is that the people who are most anxious to do good are often the ones who know least how to go about it.

The communists, who wish to destroy our society, know how to accomplish their destructive work with diabolical cleverness. They know the areas of importance for their evil ends. And they know very well what techniques to use.

But good men are frequently still looking for the answers to this most essential and elementary question of how best and most effectively to do good. All of us know men of good will who are consumed with an apostolic desire to do something worth-while for God and country, but who are floundering about wondering how to begin. As a priest who directs a social action school for laymen once commented to me: "The questions I'm most often asked by my graduates are, 'What can I do? Where am I needed most?'"

This is often the position in which the dedicated layman finds himself. Even for those who might have had a course or read a book on the subject, the terms "*consecratio mundi*," "reconstruction of the social order," or "Christianizing society" do not have any relation to reality. They simply are not meaningful for most people. The layman may see that he has a special competence and a special obligation in the temporal order in society. But how, he asks, do you go about translating the theory of the lay apostolate into concrete action in the community?

The only answer is that we must understand precisely what lies behind the jargon and terminology of the lay apostolate. We must get behind the theory in order to understand the very real problems with which it deals. The terms must be made so familiar that they immediately conjure up an image and suggest a course of action.

The first step the layman must take if he wishes to bring the theory down from its ivory tower is to see himself in context. He must consider the problem of the apostolic Christian in an unchristian world. He must understand the position of the Catholic layman in the modern American community. For the answer to the question, "What is my job as a layman?" depends on a comprehension of our situation in modern American society.

And that situation is generally one in which the life of the modern community suffers from a monumental indifference on the part of the ordinary citizen—often, it must be regretted, on the part of Catholic citizens.

When we speak of the community, we usually think of our town, our city, or the section of the large metropolitan area in which we live. Actually, we are members of many communities—our neighborhood, our city, our state, our nation, even the world community. We belong to many arrangements of people with whom we share a common interest, and in this sense we can even speak of such things as our professional or economic community.

The community, then, refers to all these groupings. And to all of them we owe certain obligations to see that they run smoothly and properly. This obligation, which all citizens have, is especially intensified for the Catholic, who as a member of the Mystical Body shares deeply in the brotherhood of man under the fatherhood of God. As Catholics we should be concerned about doing more, not less, than our neighbors in the important work of building up and maintaining all these segments which comprise the American community.

Once we see ourselves in the context of the post mid-century American community, our next need is a vision and a set of tools to make that vision a reality.

The vision we need is that of a society based on cooperation among all men of good will, men who at least agree fundamentally on basic concepts of decency and fair play—what Catholics call the natural law. A society whose institutions help lead to the natural and supernatural perfection of men. A society in which Christian humanism is a living reality.

The tools we need are basically those stressed by Pope Pius XI—the reform of morals and the reconstruction of the institutions of society according to the social teachings of the church. Many of us have heard of these tools (which we examined briefly in the preceding chapter), but for most men they lack flesh on their bones and blood coursing through their veins. For that reason it is essential that we re-examine this set of tools, this basic concept, to see what it should mean to a twentieth-century Catholic layman in America.

When we contrast our vision with present-day reality, we get a rather grim picture. Today the convinced Christian is indeed a pilgrim in an alien land. We live at a time when the type of filter cigarette they smoke has more meaning in the lives of some people than does the Cross. We have but to look about to see the effects of a high divorce and juvenile delinquency rate. Prejudice and discrimination tear our society apart. Crime rates are high. Living is made difficult for the large family. Our economy is suffering from lack of cooperative organization and inflation shrinks the value of our money. And the international communist conspiracy and the imminent peril of an all-out atomic war is like a cocked revolver at our temple. Were we not sustained by the virtue of hope, we would easily be overwhelmed by the seeming impossibility of finding a way out of this dark picture.

But from the Church we get a set of clearly defined goals and a vision of what the world should look like. What we must seek is a decent society where justice and charity prevail. We must achieve what is called the common good—that is, a state in which social and human conditions allow man to live freely and decently with at least a minimum of creature comforts— so that he is free to develop his personality and become a saint if he wills it. We want to organize society in such a way that it serves both the welfare of its members and the entire community. We want to establish economic, political, and social conditions that are most conducive to a full human and spiritual development of the individual and the group.

By studying the social doctrine of the Church, particularly as stressed in the social encyclicals, we can easily see the relationship between the lay apostolate and the construction of a Christian society. One form of the lay apostolate is aimed at spiritual goals; another—the "free lay apostolate"—is usually aimed at the community or the temporal order. In their writings and addresses, the popes tell us that to set up a Christian society we must aim at two major reforms; the reform of morals and the reform of institutions.

An English priest, Father John Fitzsimons, writing in *Catholic Mind*, said: "Alongside the Christianizing influence which every Christian must exercise on people, there is a further work which they cannot neglect, namely a steady effort to Christianize all the various social organizations which make up society. So there are two arms to the apostolate. The first is a personal apostolate, the second is a social apostolate, *i.e.*, the Christianization of social institutions."

For various historical and psychological reasons, most laymen who have engaged in apostolic action in modern times have been primarily concerned with spiritual goals, the changing of individuals. Only in the time since the reign of Pope Pius X has there been a steadily growing and developing interest in what Father Fitzsimons calls the "institutional apostolate."

Since the goal of Catholic social action is to reconstruct social institutions in the light of Christian principles, we have to understand fully the concept of the institution. To begin with, we must have some knowledge of society itself, of the complex social organism within whose all-pervading atmosphere we live. The social order is not a chaotic, unorganized, "free enterprise" type of entity held together by chance. Instead, the work of society is very methodically carried out through social institutions which every society has found necessary. Every culture has developed specific ways of doing things (institutions) grouped around political, economic, educational, familial, recreational, and religious needs. A social institution is the social structure and organization which grows up around the functions man must perform to meet his basic physical, social, and spiritual needs.

The very nature of man and of social relations demands that some way of doing things be worked out to meet each of man's basic necessities. The requirements themselves are universal among all men; the particular manner of doing things will vary from time to time and place to place.

As we look closely at our own American society and analyze it, for example, we find very definite types of social organization: To meet our economic needs, we have a private enterprise system. Our basic educational needs are met primarily by an extensive public school system. Man's need for sexual union and the procreation of children is fulfilled by monogamous marriage surrounded by many customs and laws defining the rights and obligations of the marital partners and their children. Our recreation is largely passive. Our political exigencies are met by a democratic way of life with a republican form of government.

The types of social institutions we have are carefully worked out both in terms of laws and customs and generally represent a consensus of opinion accepted by the majority of our citizens. By this very acceptance they tend to form our behavior and govern it and to set up certain standards for us to follow if we want to fit comfortably into society itself without frequent conflict.

We live and work and are shaped and influenced throughout our lives by the institutional framework in which we exist. It is no denial of free will to acknowledge the simple reality that man is heavily influenced and molded by the institutions that surround him.

Cardinal Suhard was speaking of this problem in *Priests Among Men* when he said: "Present day society is characterized by a new and universal phenomenon: 'socialization.' The several community organizations of another day, guilds, cities, provinces, etc., have been succeeded by an inextricable network of collective influences and new social structures. Man is now much less alone in the face of his destiny, less alone to meditate about it, less able to desire and choose for himself. The social order of today is a complicated one. There are no more rugged individualists; each one belongs to a sphere which has its own customs, duties and mores."

And some years later in his encyclical, *Mater et Magistra*, Pope John noted: "One of the typical aspects which characterize our epoch is socialization, understood as the progressive multiplication of relations in society, with different forms of life and activity, and juridical institutionalization."

Although Pope John made it quite clear that socialization was not evil—indeed, it has many benefits—he did take note of the fact that along with the benefits "it restricts the range of the individual as regards his liberty of action. It uses means, follows methods and creates an atmosphere which makes it difficult for each one to think independently of outside influences, to work of his own initiative, to exercise his responsibility and to affirm and enrich his personality."

The problem is not that society influences us, but rather that today its influence is often negative and evil. Instead of leading us toward God, many of our institutions lead us away from our divine destiny. Ideally, the social order, through its social groups and institutions, should help man to develop physically, spiritually, mentally, and morally so as to reach his ultimate goal—heaven, union with God. Yet, in fact, it is no trick for the average person to sit down nowadays and readily compile a list of our social customs and ways of doing things that present real moral dangers for the individual.

The Australian bishops alluded to this in their 1950 pastoral letter when they said: "A prime cause of the mass suffering of the people of the twentieth century resides in the fact that the daily lives of vast numbers of men and women are dominated by organized bodies whose policies are dictated by men acting in defiance of, or in culpable ignorance of, the moral law. Sin has thus been elevated to the level of policy in certain organizations whose acts dominate the lives of entire communities. And the wages of mass sin is mass death."

It is precisely because of this grave influence of the institutions and social groupings and structures over our lives that the Church is so concerned. This is why the popes of the twentieth century have put so much emphasis on changing the social environment as well as our souls. The day is long gone when society—through the Christian orientation of its social institutions—leads men, almost automatically, to God. Instead, our society is so ordered as to make it difficult in many ways for people to reach their heavenly destiny without great struggle and hardship.

Perhaps the problem for the layman in the community today may be best expressed by Cardinal Suhard's words that the layman "may no longer content himself with humanizing and sanctifying individual lives; he owes it to himself to Christianize 'social institutions' such as his neighborhood, his class, leisure activities, culture, the movies, radio. . . .

"Take careful note of this. The salvation of persons cannot be accomplished without a certain 'salvation' of the social order. While it is true that the social order exists for persons, and not conversely, one may nevertheless say that it is civilization itself which requires spiritualization, in all its present problems and its movements, each of which constitutes, as it were, a collective reality."

Joseph Cardinal Ritter, of St. Louis, echoed these words when he told a convention of the National Council of Catholic Women in 1958 that confirmation has given us "a commission not only of personal sanctification but also of social sanctification." He pointed out that "Catholic Action or the lay apostolate is not something sectarian, but is genuinely universal. It is an action or apostolate to all contemporary society."

Once we begin to grasp the significance of how society relates to the development and growth of men, we are one step closer to our goal of a Christian society. We can then understand that it is impossible for us to reach out and touch society directly. Society is not a *thing,* a separate entity you can convert. It is actually many things, many people gathered into many types of social groupings and institutions. To reconstruct society, therefore, we must reconstruct these social groups and institutions in which people are gathered and regulated.

The Church sees the importance of institutions; she sees people caught up in a web of institutions, often not able to do what they would like. The man in a highly competitive industry. What can he do? He would like to improve working conditions and wages, but if he tried it alone he would go bankrupt. To change conditions in his industry, he must effect an institutional change. He will, in practice, have to organize the industry better: he might, for example, get all the employers to join together and *institutionalize* better working conditions and wages by agreeing on a code of fair competition that would take basic wages and working conditions out of the competitive market. He will have to work to replace a bad institution with a good one.

At this point in their understanding of the problem, many Catholics tend to throw up their hands at the immensity of the task confronting them and turn to the false security of a simplex, black and white solution. "Concentrate on converting the individuals who make up society," they say, "and society will automatically be converted as a result."

Like all easy solutions to complex problems, this answer is not so simple as it appears. The very existence of a secular society that continually exerts unchristian pressure on us is in itself a deterrent to conversion. The unreconstructed social institutions themselves are major factors militating against mass conversion. Man and society being what they are, we need to work both on individuals and the framework of the society in which they live. Both mutually affect each other. Both must be converted.

Social action is the virtue of social justice at work. Social justice requires that we work through groups to set up a society that will allow for the fullest and most profitable development of the human personality. But to reach such a goal we must engage in social action, that is, we must act to organize society so that every man will have adequate opportunity to provide for the needs of body and soul—which is another way of talking about the common good.

The goal of social action is the salvation, the sanctification of society. Its purpose is simply to organize society in such a way that it will be easy for people to lead holy lives in close union with their Saviour, unhampered by unchristian social pressures.

Social action, therefore, is not something reserved for socalled "liberal Catholics." It is part and parcel of the full Christian life. With the proper motivation, it can even be a path to sanctity; for through such action in society we can demonstrate a love for our neighbor which is the other side of the love-of-God coin.

It is essential to note that some form of group action is a fundamental part of social action. The problems involved in society are institutional by their very nature and therefore they depend on an institutional solution. A parent may be disturbed by the fact that every time he sends his child to the corner drugstore or newsstand, the child is subjected to the temptation of objectionable "girlie" magazines or lurid paperbacks.

A personal solution might be to attempt to keep the child from such influences. Obviously, this is no real answer. Instead, he must join with other parents to form a group that can offer a pressure equal to the pressure of the publishers and the distributors, within the limits of democratic processes. A group of parents is able to act more effectively to see that existing obscenity statutes are enforced and can, as a group, make their views felt.

Of course, the work of individuals is always essential and invaluable. But, ordinarily, only an organization—with its note of permanence and its ability to form public opinion and provide leadership—can deal with other groups and organizations in society.

It has been said that the personal apostolate is no longer enough today. This does not mean that we no longer require great saints; indeed, we do. Perhaps never before in history since the early centuries of Christianity has personal holiness been so desperately called for. And lay apostles who do not continually nourish their souls at the fount of the sacraments and at the Eucharistic Banquet will soon fall by the wayside in the face of the trials and tribulations which are part of every apostolic life.

But the very structure of society has changed rapidly since the Industrial Revolution. In the ordinary course of events, individuals are no longer able to change entire institutions. Instead, if they wish to change the existing social order they must band together into groups to deal with group problems. Our society has simply become too big for the ordinary person to influence more than a small slice of his environment. We live today in a world in which the voice of the individual may most effectively be heard through a powerful group or organization.

The very basis of the layman's apostolate to the community is love—love of God and of neighbor. It is a recognition that Christ wishes His creatures to live in a world that will allow them to flourish both as human beings and as sons of God. And it is an understanding of God's plan to build and sustain a Christian society through the continuing social action of His modern day apostles in the world.

Basically, with few exceptions, some form of social action in the community is for every practicing Christian. No one in the world can afford to be oblivious of society, for it is too powerful a force in man's life to ignore. And there is room for everyone's contribution to the cause, according to individual talents and opportunities.

In what we might call the *direct* social action apostolate, a comparatively small number are able to take a first-hand part in the control of socio-economic life—holding important positions and influential offices, locally, nationally, or internationally, in government, business, or unions, for example.

We can even extend this list to include those who are engaged full-time in interracial work, housing agencies, community organizations, and the like. These are the front-line soldiers in the field who can have a more or less immediate effect on society and social institutions.

Most of us, however, must content ourselves with the *indirect* social action apostolate of the layman in the community. We are the followers who can first of all inform ourselves about the social teachings of the Church. Then, in our personal contacts, we can help prepare our friends and acquaintances for the social changes those in the direct apostolate are able to accomplish. Many improvements in society which could be brought about relatively easily now die a-borning simply because public opinion is not yet ready. In the indirect apostolate, we can help prepare the way for the acceptance of a Christian society.

Closely related to this is the opportunity most of us have to take an active part in some of the many organizations which influence the life of the community. To be specific, let's spell this out by using the example of a particular individual. Let's say that he is a young, junior executive-type businessman on his way up. He is married and has several preschool-age children.

For him, the lay apostolate has three facets.

First, there is the personal apostolate of good example and prayer. This is an apostolate for every Catholic. As Pius XII has explained, because of time, ability, and other circumstances, some persons cannot take an active part in the broader lay apostolate, but they can and are obliged to set a good example and to pray for the success of the apostolate.

Second, both he and his wife share the obligation to Christianize their own family life and, according to their opportunities and abilities, the family life of others. Perhaps they belong to the Christian Family Movement or are active in some form of the marriage or family life apostolate. Both as a family and as individuals they cooperate with their pastor and take such part in parish, diocesan, or national activities as they are able.

Lastly, he and his wife might work to bring Christ into the society in which they live.

Depending on the time she has available from her primary family duties, and on her special training and abilities, his wife might take part in some group such as the League of Women Voters, the woman's auxiliary of groups to which her husband belongs, or the women's section of the political party with which they are affiliated.

The husband, too, has his responsibilities. There might be some organization within his business, profession, or industry to which he could devote himself. Or there might be need of a group which he could help initiate. Possibly a civic or fraternal group is the organization most fitting for him. Or maybe politics is his cup of tea and he begins to make a contribution on the precinct level. Conceivably his interest lies in working with the Boy Scouts or taking part in a veterans' organization.

The possibilities are limited only by the individual's position and natural interests. The problem is not to find some organization to belong to, but to select those of the many possible groups to devote your time.

Each segment of daily life needs its share of moral and institutional reform. And since it is the layman who lives in the world, it is his natural apostolate to remake that world in the image and likeness of Christian principles. Principles that will allow each man greater freedom of conscience and opportunity.

There is great need to stress the ultimate necessity of both moral and institutional reform. The need exists because it is so easy for us to become oversold on our own particular approach in the moral or institutional area. But in the long run neither a reform of morals nor a change in the social structure alone is enough.

Social justice alone is not enough; we need social charity, love of God, which makes us concerned enough about our neighbor to keep plugging away year after year at building a better life for him. And changing a person's morals is not enough if we turn around and place him right back into an unchristian society that makes it difficult for him to obey the laws of God.

This is the great wisdom of the Church: to take into account the dual nature of man, to understand and appreciate the needs of both body and soul. It is not enough to say, "Be good. Obey the laws of God."

We must also help a person to be good. In the spiritual order, the Church has the primary responsibility for this through the Sacraments, her educational system, and in thousands of other ways. And in the realm of the temporal order it is the apostolate of the layman to see that society in no way conflicts with the conscience of man, to see that society provides for man's human and religious development so that he can begin on earth the life that will reach its fruition only in heaven.

But even knowing all this theory, where do we begin in our apostolic work? To be more specific, where do *I* begin?

The place to begin is the point at which you find yourself. Pope Pius XI gave us the general approach to be followed when he said that like must go to like: workers to workers, employers to employers, lawyers to lawyers, teachers to teachers. Take stock of yourself, your position in society, your talents and abilities. In terms of the vision we have of the kind of society the Church—Christ—wants, what are the greatest needs you see? What are the greatest impediments to the fulfillment of this kind of society? Where can you be most effective in helping to correct an unjust situation or organize a group to meet an unmet need?

Begin by considering the main social institutional areas that make up our society. Take your choice. You are needed in your parish, in your union, management or professional association, your political party, in the family apostolate, in parent-school associations, and in recreational and youth work.

Specifically, you can play a part in solving the race question, one of the greatest moral and institutional problems of our times. Housing, especially for large families, is a problem in every section of our land. The increasingly large percentage of senior citizens in our nation demands our attention. It is important that we make a contribution to the field of public education. Dedicated, competent men are needed in both political parties. International organizations of many types provide a twentieth-century opportunity for building a peaceful and cooperative world community on many levels.

Everything that affects man is of interest to the apostolic layman. For love of God and neighbor, we seek to sanctify our social environment and in so doing to sanctify ourselves as well. Whether social institutions run well or badly depends on whether we accept them as they are or make our small contribution to improving and maintaining them. What is needed desperately today is for hundreds of thousands of dedicated men and women to play an effective part in seeing—directly or indirectly—that they run well.

It is like the old story of looking at the reverse side of a tapestry. From the back we see only loose ends and get only a blurred idea of the whole design. But from the front we can see the whole picture, the purpose of the work.

Except for our idea of the layman's apostolate to the community and our vision of the type of society we are working toward, most of us will never see the finished product from the front. The man who attends union meetings faithfully. The groups which dedicate themselves to informing voters so that our government has more intelligent, grass-roots democracy. The individual who fights for justice in the admission of minority groups to his fraternal organization. The woman who gives her time and talents to civic and cultural groups. The person who serves without pay on the school board. The man who goes through the deadening routine each year of helping to raise money for the work of private or community agencies. The men and women who sit patiently through untold hours of committee or organizational meetings always ready to make a helpful suggestion, always able to inspire the group to do something worth-while for the community. The businessman who seeks to raise the ethical standards of his industry.

The chances are that none of these people will see the completed tapestry of community life. But God sees it. And one day He will show it to them.

Hundreds of thousands, millions of dedicated men and women the world over, each adding a little mortar or a brick or two to the structure of a good society. They are helping to establish and maintain moral and environmental conditions which encourage the wholesome growth of the human personality. They are freeing man from injustice and tyranny—economically, politically, socially. And by freeing him they help make it possible for his soul to climb the heights of heaven.

The apostolate of the Church, and of the laymen who are the Church, is as broad and wide and deep as the needs of man. As laymen we are just beginning to sense our apostolate and its demands. The work is often difficult, the rewards are not immediately tangible. But in the midst of it all, we can be grateful for the unparalleled opportunities we have, taking for our motto the words of Pope Pius XI:

"Let us thank God that He makes us to live among the present problems . . . it is no longer permitted to anyone to be mediocre."

CHAPTER 10

Catholics in the Community

Only a few years ago, the best conversation-starter in a rectory parlor or at a Catholic meeting of any kind was to mention the "Catholic ghetto." It was sure to get a rise out of almost everyone present, for those were the days of the middle 1950s when Catholics were in the first flush of an almost morbid public examination of conscience. Many of our lay and clerical leaders were raising serious questions about our place in American life and the quality of our contribution to the commonweal.

The Catholic ghetto referred to a state in which Catholics were withdrawn or separated from the wider society in which they live. Like the Jewish ghetto of old, the Catholic ghetto is one in which Catholics have set themselves off from their neighbors. Unlike the Jewish ghetto, its Catholic counterpart is a voluntary one and is more a matter of mind than of actual physical separation.

This matter of mind is what we might refer to as the ghetto mentality. It is a mentality fostered and formed by a withdrawal or separation; and it is characterized by exclusiveness. Such a mentality may often see nothing good that is not in some way connected with the Church. It takes pride in whether a certain actor or baseball player is a Catholic. It is the kind of mentality that seeks to withdraw from the world because it feels that the world is somehow a threat to its faith and morals. It reads only Catholic magazines or books that are "safe." In short, it is the kind of mentality which is really not catholic in the universal sense but merely Catholic in the most restricted and unhealthy sectarian sense.

This whole matter of the ghetto has some logical and

clear-cut historical reasons behind it. It has left its mark on the Irish, the Germans, the Italians, the Poles, and even the present-day Puerto Ricans. When the Poles came to America, for example, they settled not on farms but in large urban areas, which were predominantly Protestant. Because they were immigrants and at the bottom of the economic ladder they banded together in physical ghettos not only to preserve their Faith but for mutual economic aid as well. Because of this mixture of circumstances as well as because of a certain amount of persecution from the non-Catholic majority, Polish Catholics for many years worked out their lives pretty well separated from the larger society in which they lived.

It is only today with the rush to the suburbs and the upward social and economic mobility of the sons and daughters of the early Polish and Irish and Italian and German immigrants that the physical ghetto is disappearing (although it is by no means entirely gone, for various Spanish-speaking groups have at least partially replaced the European immigrants). The problem that remains, however, is largely that of the ghetto state of mind. Catholics still have a historical legacy of social separation, which is not easy to shed. Thus, many Catholics—clergy and lay—find it difficult to rid themselves of a mentality which is primarily concerned with things Catholic—to the exclusion of secular or a-religious matters.

We stand today on the threshold of a new attitude on the part of younger Catholics who are being more and more indoctrinated with the ideas of the lay apostolate and the idea of witnessing in the temporal order. But we have not yet crossed that threshold and it is generally agreed Catholics are not having a proportionate impact on the social, economic, educational, and political life of America. Many Catholics today seem somewhat afraid to take the plunge and involve themselves in large numbers in the sea of civic, cultural, professional, and community groups which are not Catholic in orientation.

The figures do not seem to have changed much, for instance, since the middle 1950s when Father Thurston N. Davis, S.J., editor of *America,* wrote of the need for Catholic scholars to "mingle with colleagues of other religious faiths in their respective academic disciplines." He found, as an illustration, that only a relatively few members of the American Catholic Philosophical Association were also members of the American Philosophical Association (thirty out of 868). And following this up further, the prominent Catholic historian Msgr. John Tracy Ellis found in comparing the American Historical Association and the American Catholic Historical Association that there were only about 470 Catholic memberships, personal and institutional, among the American Historical Association's more than 6000 members.

The same situation would seem to apply in civic and community life generally, according to Dr. Jerome G. Kerwin, for many years professor of political science at the University of Chicago, where he was active for many years in civic and political movements. Dr. Kerwin has frequently pointed out that Catholics "have not taken advantage of the opportunities they have had for participation in secular society, particularly as far as civic affairs are concerned." And he has often noted how "very lonely" he felt during his thirty years in civic affairs in Chicago because so few other Catholics were interested.

He has commented: "I wonder sometimes if there hasn't been something faulty in the training and education of such Catholics . . . whether there has been a failure to bring the wonderful religious, doctrinal, philosophical teachings they have had to the point of practical application?"

I have had the same experience myself some years ago belonging to a civic group trying to promote better housing in a large metropolis. Protestants and Jews were active and well represented on the executive board, but it was all we could do to get Catholics—even Catholics whose offices were located in the immediate vicinity—to serve.

Why should this be so? Apart from the ghetto mentality, many Catholics are reluctant to take part even in nonreligious groups which are predominantly non-Catholic. Sometimes they are afraid they won't represent their Faith properly or that they might find themselves in situations which they are not prepared to handle; we all have a fear of the unknown. The ordinary Catholic interested in interracial justice, for instance, would normally feel much more at home joining a Catholic interracial group than a nondenominational one, so if he has a preference the chances are that he will affiliate himself with the Catholic group.

At the heart of many of the problems we have mentioned thus far is that many Catholics simply do not understand the need for cooperation with non-Catholics on the civic level for the attainment of worth-while community objectives. But it is imperative for us to realize that Catholics alone will not bring about the construction of a decent and just society— this is a job for all men of good will.

Pope Pius XII touched on this in his 1955 Christmas Message when he said (italics added): "It is their [that is, the Christians'] primary duty to act with a view to bringing about the return of modern society *in its organizations* to the sources made sacred by the word of God made flesh." There is no doubt that he is referring to the need of institutional as well as moral reform, a reflection of the teachings of Pope Pius XI.

In another part of the same message, Pius XII made an additional related point: " . . . let Christians group themselves together. But let them—and more so than others—remain open to every healthy undertaking and to all genuine progress and not withdraw themselves into a sealed enclosure [a ghetto] as if to preserve themselves from the world. Committed to promote the advantage of all men, let them not despise others, who, at any rate if they are submissive to the light of reason both could and should accept the teachings of Christianity at least what is based on natural law.

"Be on your guard," Pius XII continued, "against those who undervalue this Christian service to the world and oppose to it a so-called 'pure,' 'spiritual,' Christianity. They have not understood the divine institution—to begin from its fundamental principle—Christ is true God, but also true man."

In *Mater et Magistra*, Pope John had some additional important remarks to make. For example:

"Catholics in their economic-social activities often find themselves in close contact with others who do not share their view of life. In these circumstances, Our sons should be very careful that they are consistent and never make compromises on religion and morals. At the same time, let them show themselves animated by a spirit of understanding and disinterestedness, ready to cooperate loyally in achieving objectives that of their nature are good or at least reducible to good."

It is obvious that both Pope Pius and his successor are in favor of Catholic cooperation with non-Catholics in the civic community to work for the good of that community in the temporal order. Pope Pius speaks of cooperating on the basis of the natural law and Pope John says essentially the same thing. Practically speaking, they have supplied us with two basic directives—the need for cooperation and the idea of cooperating at least on the basis of the natural law to obtain good objectives.

We are never going to be able to set up a society characterized by justice and decency—two hallmarks of a society inspired by Christian principles—unless we utilize the contribution to be made by all men of good will. Take any community problem—housing, race relations, urban renewal, education, politics—and a moment's meditation will indicate that Catholics alone cannot solve them. Any real solution must be brought about by representatives of all segments of a society because all segments are affected by the problems. Just from the standpoint of numbers alone, it is obviously impossible for Catholics acting by themselves to bring about effective changes in an area where they may represent only a tenth, a quarter, or a half of the population. To achieve the dictates of justice they must rely on the cooperation and assistance of all men of principle. And this cooperation must be built on the basis of the natural law, on the basis of common decency and justice, not because "The Pope says . . ." or "The Church teaches. . . ."

A related question here is the role of specifically Catholic groups in working for the reconstruction of society. After all, if the real changes in the social order today will come primarily from working in the temporal order to reconstruct social institutions in the market place, how do groups identified as Catholic fit in? (I am thinking here primarily of specialized Catholic groups interested in social reconstruction—social action groups, interracial councils, the Christian Family Movement, Young Christian Students, Young Christian Workers, etc.)

Certainly in the matters, for instance, of housing or racial justice there is a great deal for Catholic groups to do. In *Mater et Magistra* Pope John notes that they have an indispensable job in social instruction and education. There will always be a continuing need for Catholic interracial or housing groups to educate Catholics in the Church's teachings on these matters and to inspire Catholics to take personal and social action to solve these ugly blots on community life. Further, such organizations represent an essential Catholic voice among human relations or housing groups. Just by being present they preach a silent sermon about the Church's interest in the human condition of man.

But in purely temporal or political matters, I believe the better part of valor for specifically Catholic groups is to avoid committing the group to a specific course of action. For example, I do not think Catholic groups should endorse political candidates and, unless there are clear-cut moral issues involved on which there is an official Catholic position, I believe they should avoid endorsing particular legislation.

In most such matters there is no one Catholic position to be followed and for a Catholic group to take a position in such matters can only serve to confuse the issues—particularly the relationship between Church and state. In the short run, the temptation is always present to throw the weight of our Catholic organization behind a particular candidate or bill or social reform. But in the long run there seems to be good reason to avoid the temptation and to avoid unnecessary direct involvement in civic affairs on the part of specifically Catholic groups.

This, however, it should be noted, makes it more obligatory than ever for individual Catholics to take part in the affairs of the community, bringing to the affairs of men a Christian outlook and approach.

More specifically on Catholic groups and Catholic Action, we have some advice given in an address to the Catholic men of Sidney, N.S.W., in August, 1955, by the Apostolic Delegate to Australia and New Zealand, Archbishop Romolo Carboni.

The Archbishop points out in one place: "In the attempt to give temporal realization to the social principles and directives of the Church, doctrinal competence must collaborate with technical skill. In this sphere of practical policies, programs, institutions, organizations, and so on, having the aim of giving concrete expression and actuation to Christian social principles, the apostolic mission of the Church is not ordinarily involved; here Catholics, animated by the spirit of Christ and formed in the social teachings of the Church, must act on their own responsibility and personal initiative, not formally as mandated by the Church."

He comments on the place of Catholic Action, or specifically Catholic, groups:

"Catholic Action may support and even establish such institutions as are necessary for the concrete actuation of Christian principles in the different sectors of social life. It may work furthermore in close harmony with such institutions as credit unions, consumers' cooperatives, nonparty industrial organizations, nonparty political organizations: but it is the nature of Catholic Action to keep itself, as does the Church herself, above and outside of political parties, for it is established not to defend the particular interests of any group but 'to secure the true good of souls.'

"It is fitting, too, because of the danger of confusion of their respective roles, that leaders of Catholic Action should not be at the head of other socio-industrial or socio-political organizations even though these latter are nonparty."

And to make a further distinction between specifically Catholic Action and action in the market place, Archbishop Carboni goes on to say: "Organizations of Catholics for the concrete actuation of principles in policies, programs, legislations, institutions, etc., work in the sphere of what is commonly called the 'action of Catholics' to distinguish it from that of Catholic Action."

One of the best examples of the proper distinction between Catholic Action and action by Catholics took place in a Midwestern city in which a Christian Family Movement group was discussing the problem of retarded children at one of their meetings. When it was revealed that there were no Catholic or community facilities for the education of these children in their city, the CFM group arranged for a series of public lectures by a priest-psychologist on the problems of parents of retarded children and how these problems could be solved. For these people, this was both a family and religious problem, or at least a family problem with religious overtones.

Before long these public lectures brought out a great many parents of retarded children into the open for the first time and showed how widespread the problem was. The parents began to wonder what they could do about it, so the CFM group took the initiative and organized a nonsectarian group representative of all the parents of retarded children in the community. Before too long this group established a private school for retarded children with a full-time faculty and an enrollment of about a hundred children.

At this stage, CFM stepped out of the picture, although some individual CFM members with retarded children remain on the board of the school, which is still operating over a decade later and which is now part of the United Fund in its community.

This incident reveals clearly that Catholic Action forms and directs the thinking of Catholics toward the goal of Christian service to the community. It does not seek to dominate or use the community to achieve a so-called "Catholic victory." It seeks to spread the kingdom of Christ for its own sake, not for ulterior motives. As Pius XII wrote to the French Bishops on June 1, 1945: ". . . speed the day when We may see rising from the ranks of your Catholic organizations a great number of personalities, solidly grounded in principle, thoroughly informed on the teaching of the Church, prepared to diffuse the Christian spirit within the social, economic and juridical domains; ready to protect the interests of religion by their civic and political action. We should like in a word to envisage a complete program of action based on this authentic Charity, which is indispensable for the reconstruction of a world tottering to its very foundations."

A primary purpose of Catholic Action groups is to inspire, inform, and prepare individuals for service in the community. They provide the individual or groups of individuals with the necessary inspiration and motivation, forming them in the principles and attitudes that must guide them in their action as Catholics. Catholic Action cannot and does not give them political instruction, but it does show its members how love of God must be demonstrated through love of neighbor in the community. And it helps orientate their thinking toward the needs of the local, national, and world community.

To be effective, Catholics must have a firm grasp of how they should act in the community with their non-Catholic brothers, and of the relationship between Catholic Action and action by Catholics. But perhaps most important of all, they must be made to see that by walling themselves behind a ghetto they are also keeping Christ from having an impact on modern society through their Christian action. For as Pius XI said in a letter to the Patriarch of Lisbon in 1933:

"Participation in public life involves a duty of social charity from the fact that every citizen should contribute as much as he can to the common good of his own nation. When this participation is inspired by Christian principles, great good flows from it—not only for the life of society, but for the life of religion as well."

CHAPTER 11

The Layman in a Pluralistic Society

History is a convenient tool that provides stability to the present and helps write the future. The statesman dealing with modern problems often looks to the past to guide him in deciding on a future course of action. The traditions and past history of many of our modern institutions—universities, businesses, armed forces—provide them with underpinnings for today and pathways toward tomorrow. Even the parent, faced with a problem with his children, calls on his own experience as a child to provide him with clues as to how he should resolve his present difficulties.

It is a lack of these common kinds of history and experience that makes so acute today the problem of the layman in our pluralistic society. American Catholics are facing problems unknown to their forefathers. Today's laymen have little past experience on which to base their future actions, so they stand apprehensively and hesitantly before the present and the future.

Some laymen, unable to cope with attempting to live a full Christian life in pagan surroundings, have drifted out of the Church and have adopted a lowest-common-denominator kind of secularism as an easy solution; they do not reject God, but they live and act as if He did not exist. Others, fearful of their irreligious surroundings, have built up what has come to be called a "ghetto mentality," and have sought to withdraw from much of modern society, erecting a kind of barricade between themselves and the world.

This pluralistic society, which confronts the layman today and which has had so much effect on him, has been pithily described by John Cogley in a commencement address at St.

John's College, Collegeville, Minnesota, in June, 1959. He
spoke of ". . . the society in which we all live; where we are
all equal before the law, Protestants, Catholics, Jews and non-
believers; the society which permits maximum liberty of choice
for its citizens; the society where Church and State are kept
separate; where the press is free to print anything it likes
within the legal bounds of libel and obscenity; where protection against any governmental infringement of personal liberty
is assured by the Constitution; where no one speaking with
the authority of the State is empowered to define the truth,
declare an orthodoxy in philosophy and theology, or say: 'You
must believe this and disbelieve that or you are anathema.' . . .
the society which, in the last analysis, can agree only on the
proposition that its members disagree, and disagree strongly,
on questions that matter most in life."

This kind of society is a new experience without historical
precedent for most American Catholic laymen who are only
a few generations removed from an immigrant background.
Frequently, their parents or grandparents, upon arrival in the
United States, sought out their own former countrymen.
Italian, Polish, German, Irish and other nationality groups set
up their own little communities within the American cities in
which they settled. They found economic, political, cultural,
and religious stability and security in these little reproductions
of the old country. It helped make the transition easier and
generally proved to be a good thing.

These communities served as kind of a compression chamber
in which the new immigrant could gradually become accli-
matized and adjusted to a new way of life within the framework of friendly and familiar surroundings. They also helped
preserve the faith of the immigrants who frequently brought
their own priests with them to minister to their spiritual needs.

But, of course, the inevitable happened. The first and
second generation children of these immigrants, for a variety of
reasons which have been widely discussed in many books, began to leave their immigrant homes and move on to other
parts of the city or nation. The sociological processes of as-

similation and accommodation were hard at work making them into full-fledged Americans.

Along with the cultural accommodations he made, the Catholic had to reach some basic decisions in regard to his religious beliefs. As we noted above, some slipped out of the Church and into secularism. Others eagerly left the physical and cultural surroundings of "the old neighborhood," but they were unwilling to desert their religion. As a solution, they built up a kind of psychological religious ghetto to protect themselves from the contamination of secularism; they avoided too much contact with secular organizations, for example, and often built their leisure activities around parochial organizations.

Since the end of World War II, however, two new historical facts have coalesced to place today's American Catholic layman in a position of crisis which he must resolve without the aid of any past history on which to draw for assistance. For the problems he faces are unique and he will find little in ancient or modern history to supply him with the answers he needs.

World War II itself helped tear millions of young men from their social and cultural roots and throw them, unprotected, into close and prolonged contact with other young men of every cultural, religious, political, and economic background. Then, from 1946 on, as young Catholics returned from the wars, married, and established families, the housing shortage made it necessary for many of them to scatter far from their origins to find adequate living quarters. For the first time, many found themselves uprooted not only from their socio-cultural moorings but from their religious roots as well. The dramatic growth of groups such as the Christian Family Movement at about this time is an indication of the strong desire on the part of many couples to solve this problem by seeking out like-minded religious couples who would help them reinforce their religious values.

But about the same time the voice of the Church grew more and more insistent—we must withdraw from the ghetto and penetrate modern society with the principles of Christ. For too long have we ignored the secular world. It is the layman's job to restore that world to Christ. And the only way to do this is to become a part of it.

This is where the layman stands today—trying to work out some system of life that will make it possible for him to remain unstained by the world's secularism and paganism and at the same time allow him to become a dynamic and spiritually alive part of that world. Since most laymen are married and because the problem is particularly acute for those who are responsible for the formation of children—the laity of the next generation—I shall concentrate on this problem as it affects the Christian family.

Religion aside, our open, pluralistic society makes it very difficult for the family life of any distinctive minority to survive. For the norms and values of such minorities are usually so different from the norms and values of the majority that they require a conscious and sustained effort on the part of the minority to maintain itself. This is particularly true of the Catholic minority, where the standards and requirements—easily seen, for example, in the case of contraception—are much more demanding than those of the majority culture.

The Jesuit family sociologist, Father John L. Thomas, in his book, *The American Catholic Family*, explains the problems minorities face when he writes:

"Conformity tends to produce conformity in a society where there is rather general agreement on ultimate values, family standards and related behavioral patterns. People agree on how they ought to act in various social situations, and when deviations occur from approved standards of conduct, the offender is punished by loss of esteem or by the imposition of more positive sanctions. At the same time, conformity is rewarded so that, under such circumstances, to conform almost constitutes the path of least resistance for the individual. . . .

"A minority which represents a distinct cultural subsystem in a pluralistic society, however, cannot rely on the current social mechanisms in securing conformity to its family standards. Hence, it is faced with a threefold task. It must develop means for assuring adequate knowledge of its family standards by group members. Since knowledge does not necessarily lead to conformity, effective motivation must be maintained. And, finally, there must be sufficient solidarity among group members to supply the mutual support which is lacking in the dominant society."

If we examine the threefold task confronting us as a minority group, we can find little reason to rejoice.

The family, the school, and the Church are the traditional means by which "adequate knowledge of its family standards" are passed on to each new generation of the Catholic minority. Unfortunately, the current trend is for parents to abdicate their role as religion teachers and to turn this over to the school; and making the situation even more serious is the fact that the growth of the Catholic population is making it more and more difficult for Catholic children to get a Catholic education from kindergarten to college. And, although the Church is doing a valiant job through the Cana and pre-Cana Conference technique, this approach is still in its infancy in many places.

Effective motivation depends on many factors—parents, the spiritual direction of skilled priests, and to a large extent on a meaningful participation in the Church's liturgical life, which opens up channels of grace and wisdom. However, the shortage of religious vocations means that the priests we have will be able to devote less and less time to the time-consuming work of spiritual direction. And we are far behind in most places in making the liturgy the center of our religious lives.

Finally, mutual support becomes more difficult as Catholics, like other Americans, move more and more frequently from one place to another, often becoming isolated from fellow Catholics as they tend to become more a part of the secular culture—the pluralistic society—which engulfs them.

Yet, I do not think these problems are the real danger we face, for in what era have Christians not been surrounded by difficulties? Some have faced greater problems, some less. But if anything distinguishes the Christian, it is that for him life is always a matter of warfare, whatever his time or clime.

I, for one, do not fear our problems so much as I do the kind of malaise I sometimes detect on the part of some Catholics who shrug their shoulders and halfheartedly ask, "Yes, but what can we do about it?" We are developing a defeatist attitude that is more concerned with problems than with opportunities. We sometimes seem to be so worried about plugging the holes on what appears to be a sinking ship that we forget to maintain the vessel on its course and keep moving ahead. We are neglecting the essential Christian virtues of hope and fortitude in the face of tribulations.

Our frame of mind is crucial. Of course we must deal with problems, but there are many ways of doing this. The paranoiac sees problems as a threat; the emotionally healthy person sees them as obstacles to be overcome, as challenges to action and opportunities for good—not as something that should frighten us. It is essential for the survival of our minority in a pluralistic society that we spend more time developing this latter attitude in our entire approach to the challenge of living a Christian life in an unchristian world.

Listen to the words of a Dutch writer quoted in William J. Whalen's *Catholics on Campus*, whose words have relevance here. He wrote: "Many of us speak and act as if we considered it obvious that a Catholic who ventures into a non-Catholic milieu will naturally lose his faith. If anything is natural it is that in such circumstances the non-Catholic milieu is in great danger of losing its unbelief."

It is this attitude, it seems to me, that must form our attitude and approach as we examine the challenges and opportunities for the Christian family today.

One of the most immediate challenges is how to counter secularism. As Catholic parents, we are especially concerned about the effect of a pagan atmosphere on the spiritual formation of our children. Because our society is one characterized by religious pluralism, we simply have to face up to the fact that we and our children will always be associating with many different groups with widely varying sets of values and religious ideas. We do not live in a society that strongly reinforces the religious life of the family.

Parents know well what this means. They have to make certain minimal demands on their children—attendance at Mass at least on Sunday, time for confession on Saturdays, possibly some family devotions or other religious activities. If they are living in a neighborhood of secularists, or even among Catholics who don't make these similar demands, their children may rebel or they may be inclined to think that religion can't be too important because the other people they know don't take it seriously. When an individual Christian family is isolated in the midst of a nonreligious society, it is difficult to rear the children properly.

There are a variety of ways we can react to this common situation. We can throw up our hands in resignation, make as few demands as possible on our children, and hope for the best. Another defeatist approach would be to attempt to keep our children from associating with their non-Catholic neighbors—an impractical solution at best.

The person who regards this challenge as an opportunity, however, will take time to think the problem through and arrive at a balanced solution.

One small group of families in a Midwestern diocese has taken a radical step and has formed its own community, buying land together and helping each other build family-oriented homes. These families are not seeking to withdraw from society or to keep their children from meeting people who are different from them. They only want their children to know enough people who are *like them*. A child can stand to know that some people disagree with his parents. What shakes his confidence is the discovery that *everybody* disagrees with them.

It is important to understand, incidentally, that the people involved in this community have not withdrawn from the world about them. They have stepped aside from the fast and furious flow of some of American life in order to have more time to build a Christian family and to be able to live and work more completely with their children. But the parents are active in community life, both in Catholic and in secular projects. And they use every opportunity to interest their children in the idea of Christian service to the world.

Their children are not isolated from the world; rather, they are protected from some of its more deleterious influences until the children have been formed, under the protecting eye of their parents, into more mature Christians able to cope with the temptations of this world. This is not living in a ghetto mentality—at least in this case the parents involved are anything but ghetto Catholics.

Assuming that such a radical step as setting up our own Christian community is impossible for most of us, there is still much we can learn from such a group and their experience of well over a decade in total Christian family living.

For one thing, what can we do to avoid the problem of being isolated in a pagan atmosphere? One thing we all certainly can do is to seek out the companionship of like-minded Christian families with whom our children may associate. This will help give the children the balance they need to see that many other families share their parents' views and ideas.

There is also the possibility in these days of frequent moves to the suburbs for concerned Catholic families to buy homes near each other so they can form their own little community within the larger community. The important thing is for families who share the same ideals to join together so they give each other and their children the mutual support and encouragement that comes with unity of purpose.

Note carefully that this is not fostering a ghetto mentality, which is essentially a negative, defeatist withdrawal from the majority culture. Instead, what I am suggesting is a positive protection on the level of ideals and religious practices. This is an essential for the Catholic minority to survive the assaults of what has been called our post-Christian society.

I am not saying that the Catholic family owes nothing to society or that we can withdraw our Christian influence from the larger community. I believe the exact opposite to be true. What I am saying, however, is that we cannot throw the doors of our homes open indiscriminately to the avalanche of pagan ideas and customs that prevail in most areas today. If our homes are to become true nurseries of the Faith, little churches in which the Holy Family dwells, we cannot allow them to be infiltrated and penetrated by paganism.

We are dealing with impressionable children, not with fully formed and mature Christians who can and must bring Christ into the secular market place without great danger of staining themselves. Until the child becomes a mature person and especially a mature Christian, we must protect him from the alluring temptations of the pagan world, all the time preparing him intelligently for the day when he must take his place in that world. But in the meantime, we must avoid the heavy doses of indifferentism that can be a serious occasion of sin for the developing character of young children.

It must be carefully understood that in urging parents to protect their children from the undue influence of the majority culture patterns until they are able to stand on their own two feet spiritually and intellectually, I am not suggesting that the children be removed from reality. I certainly cannot approve, for example, of that kind of child training or education that never discusses evil or pretends that it does not exist. This is as dangerous in the moral sphere as it is in the physical sphere for parents not to warn their children that they shouldn't accept candy or rides from strangers.

The child must certainly be made aware of evil, but he does not have to experience it personally to understand it. And it is primarily the parents' responsibility to see that the child's knowledge of such matters is suited to his own individual development.

The great challenge, the great opportunity facing Catholic parents today is how to strike the right balance between being a *closed* family on the level of the formation of their children and at the same time to be an *open* family, a family that develops in its children the great concepts of the Mystical Body and our obligation to Christianize the community.

It is being done. It can be done. The challenge that faces

each of us is how to do it, how to help the secular milieu lose some of its unbelief. One thing we can be certain of is that as we solve this problem we shall also be solving some larger problems as well. For just as the early Christian communities grew by drawing pagan individuals into their strongly religious life, so too will we grow by building up a firm Christian family life that will attract and convert others.

In our concern for the life of the minority in a pluralistic society, however, it is essential for us to keep our perspective. That is, such a society is not an unmitigated evil. It has advantages as well as disadvantages. The political benefits, for instance, are incomparable and every American Catholic accepts and supports our government and Constitution, which for us are among God's choicest blessings. And being a minority has its compensations, for this tends to make us think more often and more intelligently about our religious convictions and values and often helps to strengthen our Faith and bolster our beliefs.

A cursory glance back through history, or even at today's experience, demonstrates that all too often state religions of the majority can easily become whited sepulchers with all the outer trappings but none of the inner vitality needed to make faith a reality in our lives. The very fact that the Catholic Church in America has flourished in the midst of such a society should readily suggest to even the most casual observer that in the long run the free and open society might well be the best for religion.

Our aim, therefore, is not to change the basic, fundamental political structure of the pluralistic society or to develop an antagonism toward it on the part of our children. Our special concern as a religious minority is to work toward a change in the moral climate of our society. To achieve this goal we intend to use the tools of the pluralistic society—persuasion, discussion, and rational debate. And our arms will be the Christian weapons of truth and love.

We are now writing the history which may well be the guide and inspiration of future generations and which may provide our children and their children with the experience they need to make their religion a vital force in their own generation and to hand it down, vibrant and living, to the next. On what we do or fail to do in our lifetime may well depend the future of the Catholic minority in our pluralistic society for centuries to come.

CHAPTER 12

Catholics and Democracy

More than any other event in American history, the 1960 presidential campaign served to focus attention on the problem of the relations between Church and state and the position of Catholics in a democracy. For even though the campaign and defeat of Al Smith had also aroused many of the same questions, the issue has much more relevance in our generation because of the growing strength of Catholicism in the United States and the development of a better educated and more articulate laity. Many of the questions that occupied the minds of non-Catholic Americans in 1928 were primarily academic; today, many of them are far less so.

What the average Protestant did not realize at that time and even now, however, is that most Catholics were as confused and bewildered by the whole affair as were those outside the Catholic Church. The great majority of Catholics in the United States simply did not realize that any problems existed and at first, at least, they could not understand what all the shouting was about. Most American Catholics simply took their position in America for granted as they did their patriotism and love of our democratic institutions. Indeed, many of them were just as badly shaken up as were most Protestants by the statement of the Puerto Rican bishops just before the election, which told Puerto Rican Catholics not to vote for one of the political parties running in that American dependency.

The first, almost intuitive, reaction of many Catholics to the questions leveled at Mr. Kennedy and the Church was that anti-Catholicism was behind the queries. As time went on, however, Catholics began to see the problems in the minds of their Protestant friends for the first time, problems that often were real ones for the non-Catholic.

Even today, perhaps the most important single question in the mind of even friendly non-Catholics has to do with the sincerity of the Church's acceptance of democracy. They do not question the sincerity of the individual American Catholics they know, but the question in their minds goes something like this: Do the feelings of American Catholics really represent the mind of the Catholic Church? After all, who speaks for the Church? We are able to find statements by Catholic churchmen in modern times which take the view that if Catholics ever become a majority in a country they will suppress much of the religious freedom of non-Catholics. And then we look at many "Catholic" countries today, such as Spain and certain Latin American nations, and we find our worries justified. We would like to believe our American Catholic neighbors, but we do have legitimate reasons for our fears.

In many years of intimate association with both the official and unofficial Church on many levels, this writer has never found any reason to doubt that the average American Catholic bishop, priest, or layman is anything but enthusiastic for the American way of life, nor would they change it if they could. But it is also a fact that there is no official statement from the Vatican that religious liberty and tolerance is the Catholic ideal and the goal toward which Catholics should strive whether they are a majority or not.

It is likewise true, of course, that there is no official statement to the contrary. The present situation is that this matter has simply not been decided one way or another by the Church. It is still an open question, although there are two major views held by those who have discussed the issue: One view is substantially that feared by most Protestants. The other is what has come to be called the "American" view, though in fact it is widely held by many non-Americans as well. This view stands for tolerance and would find no difficulty in accepting the present American arrangement; indeed, some of its proponents would eagerly make their own the words of James Cardinal Gibbons, Archbishop of Baltimore, in 1909:

"American Catholics rejoice in our separation of Church and State; and I can conceive of no combination of circumstances likely to arise which would make a union desirable either to Church or State. We know the blessings of our present arrangement; it gives us liberty and binds together priests and people in a union better than that of Church and State. Other countries, other manners; we do not believe our system adapted to all conditions; we leave it to Church and State in other lands to solve their problems for their own best interests. For ourselves, we thank God we live in America, 'in this happy country of ours,' to quote Mr. [Theodore] Roosevelt, where 'religion and liberty are natural allies.'"

So, as we have seen, there are two views prevalent in the Church today: One would tend to ally the Church with the state and put legal restrictions on religious minorities. In practice, this view would seem to desire the Church to achieve substantially the same position it now holds in Spain. The other view, certainly equally respectable, would grant religious minorities complete civil freedom and would not wish a Church and state alliance. It would agree with the reasoning of Cardinal Carejeria, Patriarch of Lisbon, who said about the Concordat between the Vatican and Portugal:

"The Portuguese State recognizes the Church as she is, and ensures her freedom; but she does not support or protect her as a state established religion. . . . What the Church loses in official protection, she gains in virginal freedom of action. Free from any liability toward political power, her voice gains greater authority upon consciences. She leaves Caesar a complete clear field in order for herself better to attend to the things that are of God. She is the pure crystal from which the treasure of the Christian revelation is streaming forth."

The next question, of course—and one of great interest to the American Catholic layman—is: Which of the two views is likely to become the official view of the Church when the

whole matter is finally settled? Which view has more—and
more powerful—adherents?

To answer the second part first, I am aware of no statistics
available to be able to give an intelligent reply. And secondly,
it would certainly be rash of anyone at this stage (or any stage)
to attempt to read the mind of the Church in advance. But
if we may judge from the public statements that have been
made in recent years, and which are being made today by the
highest churchmen, the so-called American view is certainly
receiving many commendations in whole or in part.

That this is not merely wishful thinking is made clear by a
recent study by a non-Catholic, Dr. A. F. Carrillo de Albornoz,
a research specialist at the Geneva headquarters of the World
Council of Churches. In his survey of *Roman Catholicism
and Religious Liberty*, which appeared in *Catholic Mind*, Dr.
Carrillo comments:

"Roman Catholic literature representing this modern tendency has lately been so voluminous and of such quality that it
would be an understatement to say that, for *one* book or
article in favor of the traditional doctrine, *ten* have been published defending universal religious freedom as 'thesis'; and
we should note that they have all been published with the
'nihil obstat' of the Roman Catholic authorities. As is well
known, the 'nihil obstat' does not always mean that the book
approved reflects exactly the official Roman Catholic doctrine
on the matter, but it does always mean that nothing in such
book is against the official teaching of the Roman Catholic
Church."

And he concludes: "We think that there is evidence enough
of the fact that:

"1. Many Roman Catholic theologians, in many countries,
defend a new theory in favor of complete religious freedom in
principle. . . .

"2. This theory has in no way been condemned but, on the
contrary, is supported by very important numbers of the Roman Catholic Hierarchy; and

"3. This theory is not a tactical variant of the old doctrine for reasons of opportunism, but another radical and irreducible doctrinal position which is very sincerely and fiercely fighting the old one."

One of the major reasons for the development and spread of this "new theory" has been the very existence of the United States and the emergence of some new nations along similar lines. There was in the medieval past never any real reason to question the relationship of the Church to the state when the citizens of the state were almost without exception Catholic. After the Reformation, the nations—Protestant or Catholic —continued with an established Church or at least a dominant Church. The United States was really the first modern state to be neutral toward religion, but at the same time friendly to all beliefs; it was a new experience in religious history. Then, as the Roman Catholic religion grew and flourished within this new type of Church-state relationship, as American Catholic churchmen accepted and praised it, it became more and more apparent to many that this was not only a legitimate but a very desirable type of coexistence.

But even as this becomes more and more apparent it is not outside the realm of possibility that the Catholic Church may never issue an official statement taking one side or the other in the discussion. The Church is a great respecter of individuality and seeks always to allow individuals—persons or nations —the right to develop their own ways of social life and institutions, so long as these do not conflict with the laws of God. The Church does not say that one type of government or one kind of society is better than another; she condemns only the immoral and allows man the right to make his own choice of the many possible political, social, and economic arrangements that may be set up in accordance with the laws of God.

The basic principles that the Church insists on in any relationship between Church and state are few and simple in conception. As stated by the distinguished Jesuit theologian, Father Gustave Weigel, in a talk in Washington, D.C., in September, 1960, they are: "First, the sacral [the spiritual order or the Church] is the last and highest dimension of man

whereby he is in contact with divinity. Its imperatives are absolute and ultimate. Secondly, on a lower and more immediate
plane the state is necessary for man and it is God-willed. On
its own plane of action and existence, the state is autonomous
and authoritative without making it superior to the sacral
which is of a distinct and higher order. Thirdly, for the good of
man who is simultaneously in the dimension of the sacral and
in the dimension of the secular, there should be the highest
possible concord between the two orders of command, a concord which, however, will never mean identity."

It is immediately quite clear, though, that an almost infinite
variety of social institutions might be initiated which would
fulfill these requirements—from the American democracy to a
constitutional monarchy to a benevolent dictatorship. The
Church does not intervene in the choice men make except
to point out when the state interferes with the fundamental
natural and religious rights of men. If she did otherwise, she
could easily be accused of interfering in the temporal order—
which is the domain of the state—and although at times we
might wish her to speak more quickly and more often about
certain types of governments, I think in the long run history
will demonstrate her wisdom of not speaking unless her intervention is clearly needed.

This view, it must be admitted, is not very satisfactory to
non-Catholics. The American Catholic layman soon learns
in any discussion of Church and state that what most non-
Catholics would like to have on the record is a once-for-all,
ironclad, official statement affirming the desirability of the
"American" view of Church-state relations. But because for
the reasons discussed above such a statement does not seem
likely to be immediately forthcoming, the American Catholic
lay leader should be aware of the growing amount of authoritative material on the need for religious toleration.

Often quoted, for example, is Pope Pius XII's December 6,
1953, address to Italian Catholic jurists on the world community and religious tolerance. In one part of this address,
speaking of how in a world community of many and no re-

ligious beliefs it would be possible for these nations and opinions to coexist, he proposes this "rule or ordinance":

"Within its own territory and for its own citizens, each state shall regulate its religious and moral affairs according to its own laws; nevertheless, throughout the whole territory of the international community, the citizens of each member-state shall be allowed to exercise their own beliefs and ethical and religious practices, insofar as these practices do not violate the penal laws of the state in which they are residing."

In another place in the same address he comments:

"Reality shows that error and sin are in the world in great measure. God reproves them; yet He permits them to exist. Therefore the affirmation that religious and moral error must always be impeded whenever possible, because to tolerate them is in itself immoral—is not valid unconditionally and absolutely.

"Moreover, God has not even given to human authority such an absolute and universal command, in matters of faith and morals. The common conviction of mankind, Christian conscience, the sources of revelation, and the practice of the Church have never recognized the existence of such a command.

"We omit here other scriptural texts in support of this argument, except that of Christ in the parable of the Cockle which gives the following admonition: Let the cockle grow in the field of the world together with the good seed, in view of the harvest (Matt. 13:24–30). The duty to suppress moral and religious error cannot, therefore, be an ultimate norm of action. It must be subordinated to higher and more general norms which, under certain circumstances, permit and may even make it appear that the best choice for promoting greater good is the toleration of error."

More recently, Giacomo Cardinal Lercaro, Archbishop of Bologna, has written in *The Catholic Mind*, on "Religious Toleration in Catholic Tradition" and has spelled out more clearly the place of such toleration in Catholic thinking:

"The idea of tolerance as exposed in Catholic thought is

extremely simple. In substance it can be reduced to this: *no one should be forced against his will to accept the Catholic faith.* Respect for the truth demands freedom of consent. A truth imposed is not a truth accepted as such. Persuasion, Rosmini rightly noted, cannot be forced.

"With this in mind we can now turn to a consideration of the greater good which justifies religious tolerance on the part of the Catholic—namely *the need for truth to be accepted as truth.*"

This background established, His Eminence goes on to explain his point in more detail:

"What we mean is this: when one affirms that truth is objective, by that very fact he admits of a distinction between truth itself and the act by which the individual yields to truth. Hence in recognizing the objectivity of truth, the individual is, at the same time, establishing the right to personal freedom. Where truth is imposed there arises confusion between religion and politics. As history has so often demonstrated, truth tends to become an instrument in the hands of the state. According to the Christian conscience the relationship of politics to religion is one of subordination. But where truth is imposed, religion and politics become entangled. This confusion of religion and politics has been typical of every form of paganism and reflects a situation which has been carried to extremes in the totalitarian regimes of today."

Cardinal Lercaro also makes an important distinction between dogmatic and civil intolerance. On the one hand, he notes the Church is the possessor of truth and can never take the position that truth is relative or that one religion is as good as another. This does not mean, though, that the person who will not tolerate on the intellectual level dogmas he believes to be false should also be intolerant on the "civil or practical" level. Indeed, he speaks approvingly of "this principle that the positive promotion of the common good demands civil and religious tolerance. . . ."

Another remarkable statement on this subject, which demonstrates the universality of the Church's respect for individual freedom, was made in a pastoral letter issued by Cardinal Rugambwa and the archbishops and bishops of Tanganyika. The letter, on the general theme of the position of Catholics in a pluralistic society, noted that "the state has as its primary duty the fostering of the common good of society. . . . The state must in a real way acknowledge God in its work, must recognize the belief of its citizens in God and an acceptance of the order of natural law. The state has the duty of fostering religion.

"However, the state has no rights over the religious convictions of its citizens. It must guarantee freedom of religion. This guarantee implies several things: first, that the state cannot force any citizen to practice a religion and perform the acts of a cult repugnant to his conscience; secondly, in acquitting itself of its responsibilities toward the public, the state must do so in the best interests of all and with complete impartiality as regards beliefs and religions; finally that no public servant has any right to show himself biased in favor of his co-religionists in the carrying out of his duties; still less is he entitled to take advantage of his position as a servant of the public to favor unduly the organs of any particular religious persuasion. . . ."

But what, the letter asks, about the position of the Catholic Church? Should it receive any special treatment from the state because its members believe it to be the one, true Church? The letter answers:

"We firmly believe that the state will best help the Catholic Church by not forcing the conscience and the freedom of religion on the one hand, and by pursuing the common good on the other. This pursuit of the common good will in effect create the temporal milieu most favorable to the workings of God's grace. It will help to bring about those fundamental conditions of justice, order and peace which are necessary for men who are called to the divine life, to fulfill their destiny. It will bring about those conditions most favorable to a sincere, free, truly human search for the Truth. . . ."

Closer to home, the question might well be raised: What

about Catholics and the Church in America? Do they really believe in democracy? Or will things be different when and if they become a majority? The answer to that question is to be found in the words and the deeds of American Catholics throughout our history.

It was a favorite argument of many of Mr. Kennedy's supporters during his campaign to point to the Catholic heads of state in Europe, notably France, Germany, and Italy, and observe that they were not told how to run their nation by the Vatican, so why should Americans fear that the trend was going to be reversed by the election of an American Catholic? While this is certainly a legitimate argument, it might have been somewhat more germane to stay on our own shores and point to the remarkably good record of American Catholics in regard to liberty and Church-state relations generally.

We need go no further than Maryland and Catholic Lord Baltimore's liberal attitude toward religious freedom and tolerance. As President Eisenhower noted in 1959 in a message to a meeting celebrating the 325th anniversary of its founding, all Americans "owe a debt of gratitude to the founders of Maryland who welcomed settlers of every creed to her hospitable shore." After a considerable number of Protestants came to this colony, however, they became strong enough to pass in 1704 "An Act to Prevent the Growth of Popery," which imposed many civil disabilities on the Catholics of Maryland.

The record also shows that a Catholic, Charles Carroll, signed the Declaration of Independence, and that Catholics served with distinction in our Revolutionary War and with valor and honor in all the wars in which this nation has engaged; and not the least of the men who have done so is Mr. Kennedy himself.

Because of the prestige value and almost mystic significance attached to the office of the presidency, much has been made of the ability of a Catholic to serve in that office without pressure from Church authorities. But what, we might ask, about the thousands of elective and appointive offices, from local dog catcher to the state and federal legislatures, governorships, departments of local, state, and federal government, the Supreme Court, the President's Cabinet, the military, and all the other positions in which Catholics have and do serve? Has there been any cause for real concern on the part of non-Catholics about the manner in which Catholics have and do conduct themselves in these vital governmental positions? The record is undeniably clear that Catholics have been as free from interference on the part of their Church as have any non-Catholics in similar positions.

To be more specific, take the case of the United States Supreme Court, which has had six Catholics on it, including two chief justices—Roger Taney, Edward White, Joseph McKenna, Pierce Butler, Frank Murphy, and William Brennan. Our highest judicial body is certainly a key spot by which to judge the record of Catholics on Church-state relations.

In his speech on the religious issue before the American Society of Newspaper Editors before his election, Mr. Kennedy asserted that ". . . our highest Court . . . has a long history of Catholic Justices, none of whom, so far as I know, was ever challenged on the fairness of his rulings on sensitive Church-state relations."

"Is this assertion justified?" asked three non-Catholics—Harold W. Chase, a professor of political science at the University of Minnesota and two of his assistants, Margaret Jane Gree, and Robert Mollan. After a careful study of the history of Catholics on the Supreme Court, they published "Catholics on the Court" in *New Republic*: ". . . the most obvious conclusion is that the ideas of the Catholic Justices as a group are not distinguishable from the ideas of non-Catholics. Indeed, the record of Justice Murphy alone is enough to belie the contention that every devout Catholic must necessarily feel compelled to give precedence to Catholic doctrine over the constitutional doctrine of separation of church and state."

Some non-Catholics in the face of a statement such as this may tend to wonder if Catholics in positions of public office and trust are not somehow less Catholic for their defense of liberty. And even some Catholics may speculate if these men are not conforming a little too much to the secular environment in which they have found themselves. In point of fact nothing could be further from the truth and the reasons why are worthy of some brief consideration.

As we have seen, the goals of the Church are supernatural and the state is concerned primarily with the temporal common good. Each is autonomous and supreme within its own sphere and while each should cooperate for the benefit of the citizen and believer who is at one and the same time a member of both the Church and the state neither may interfere in the other's domain.

Fortunately, for reasons we have discussed earlier, the Church in the normal course of events does not get into specifics. Accordingly, the Catholic politician or the appointed official or the Supreme Court Justice is free to choose an almost infinite variety of possible courses of action in his field, any one of which would be in keeping with the Ten Commandments and the doctrine of the Church. Because most issues are gray rather than black or white, you will find variety in opinions depending on the social, economic, geographic, educational and cultural background of the Catholic in public life. There is no single standard by which it is possible to judge the "catholicity" of a Catholic in public life; for as you can easily see two equally devout men may well be on opposite sides of the same issue and never for a moment diminish their personal or social sanctity.

The only yardstick by which the Catholic politician may be judged was summarized by a professor turned politician, Senator Eugene J. McCarthy of Minnesota, who in his book, *Frontiers in American Democracy* stated: "The Christian in politics should be judged by the standard of whether through his decisions and actions he has advanced the cause of justice and helped, at least, to achieve the highest degree of perfection possible in the temporal order."

The point is, of course, that it is virtually impossible for a person to pick out a "Catholic line" that members of the Church in public life are supposed to be following or to attempt to show how the Church has any undue influence on its members in the performance of their civic duties. Perhaps the most that can be done is to show what Catholics would *not* do, but once you get away from the Decalogue you would be rather hard-pressed to prove your point. Once you move from the area of principles into that of prudential judgment in applying principles in the temporal order, the record clearly shows that you will find not only Catholics but Protestants and Jews as well on every side of almost every issue.

In summary, the record of Catholics in America shows they have probably infringed less on the separation of Church and state than have their non-Catholic fellow citizens. Catholics did not pass the Volstead Act; they did not put the birth control laws on the books in Massachusetts and Connecticut; nor have they been responsible for most of the blue laws in effect in the fifty states. And it is no secret that one of the main reasons why the Catholic parochial school system exists in the United States is because even today in many parts of our nation the public schools are primarily Protestant schools in tone and in actual religious practices.

This is not to say that Catholics have been lily white in the matter of Church-state relations. Too often they have been guilty of unwise picketing of movie houses; they have not been unimportant in keeping the birth control laws on the books in some states; and they have on occasion used power politics on the local level to achieve religious goals. But in the final balance, they have been no worse than other religious groups and they have probably been better than most.

We have taken a look at the deeds of Catholics in America; now here is a short summary of some of the more significant statements by Church officials on the subject of Church-state relations with which every American should be familiar.

Back in 1787, in the *Columbian Magazine*, Archbishop John Carroll, founder of the American Catholic hierarchy, wrote: "Freedom and independence, acquired by the united efforts, and cemented with the mingled blood of Protestant and Catholic fellow citizens, should be equally enjoyed by all."

In an address in 1824, the first Bishop of Charleston, John England, proclaimed: "May God long preserve the liberties of America from the union of any church with any state! In any country, with any religion, it is an unnatural increase of the power of the executive against the liberties of the people!"

Skipping to the present, we find that in 1948 the powerful Administrative Board of the National Catholic Welfare Conference issued the following statement through its chairman, Archbishop John T. McNicholas: "We deny absolutely and without any qualification that the Catholic bishops of the United States are seeking a union of Church and State by any endeavors whatsoever, either proximate or remote. If tomorrow Catholics constituted a majority in our country, they would not seek a union of Church and State. . . . In complete accord with the Catholic doctrine, we hold firmly that our own constitutional provisions are the best for our country. Even had we the authority to do so, we would not change one iota of them."

And his successor as chairman of the Administrative Board, Archbishop Karl J. Alter, said in *Sign* magazine in July, 1960: "The fear that we as Catholics will use religious toleration here to gain the ascendancy in our country, and then, having achieved political hegemony, proceed to deprive our fellow citizens of freedom of speech in religion, of freedom of conscience, or impose our convictions upon them willy-nilly, is utterly unwarranted by any doctrine of the Catholic Church, as well as by the consistent pronouncements of the American hierarchy. We seek no privileged status; we proclaim our full adherence to the provisions of the Constitution as of now as well as for the future."

And on March 18, 1960, in an address at Loyola University in Chicago the Apostolic Delegate to the United States, Archbishop Egidio Vagnozzi, declared: "As far as the United States is concerned, I feel that it is a true interpretation of the feelings of the hierarchy and of American Catholics in general to say that they are well satisfied with their Constitution and pleased with the fundamental freedom which their Church enjoys; in fact, they believe that this freedom is to a large extent responsible for the expansion and consolidation of the Church in this great country. Whether they remain a minority or become a majority, I am sure American Catholics will not jeopardize their cherished religious freedom in exchange for a privileged position."

It would be easy to continue to multiply quotations from many additional sources, but the point has been made sufficiently that both in their words and in their deeds American Catholics have been faithful to the spirit and the letter of the American ideal of Church-state relations. By being vitally aware of their rich heritage and tradition, the American Catholic laymen of today and of the future will continue to make their distinctive contribution to the American political scene, which will both enrich and preserve it. For in a very real way, they have made their own the words of an American Catholic serviceman who, before his death in World War II, wrote his son: "Be a good Catholic and you cannot help but be a good American."

CHAPTER 13

The Layman and His Non-Catholic Neighbor

It is hardly any shift of gears at all to move from a discussion of Catholics in a democracy and Church-state relations to the area of Catholic–non-Catholic relations and the dialogue and ecumenical movement. The reason, of course, is simply that for many non-Catholics the problem of Church-state relations is the major cause of religious tensions and conflicts. It is indeed virtually impossible to enter upon a discussion of the relations among the major faiths in the United States without first exploring Catholic thinking on Church-state relations and the Catholic understanding of tolerance.

Within recent years there has been a rapid and important increase in the religious "dialogue" in the United States. On the official level, this dialogue refers to the public and private conversations which have been taking place primarily between Protestant and Catholic theologians to explore the religious matters which divide and unite Christians. Unofficially, but with the permission and encouragement of their bishops, small groups of Catholic laymen in a few places in the United States have been meeting with Protestants and Jews to talk together for the purpose of understanding each other's beliefs better.

These dialogue groups are parts of a greater whole, the whole being the ecumenical movement, which refers to all the various actions being taken by Catholics and non-Catholics to achieve ultimately a union—or reunion—among all Christians. (That is why technically, at least, it is not proper to speak of dialogue groups with Jews as part of the ecumenical movement; this comes more under the category of better religious relations among various faiths. However, in keeping with popular usage, we shall include Jews in our discussions of the dialogue.)

The ecumenical movement, of course, is not identical with the Ecumenical Council first announced by Pope John in January, 1959. The Council, however, may be looked upon as the modern culmination of current Catholic concern for unity and it will in all likelihood be a jumping-off place for an even greater Catholic interest in this important effort "that all may be one."

Among Protestants, the ecumenical movement, building on a century of efforts, has met its greatest success since the end of World War II with the formation of the World Council of Churches at Amsterdam in 1948 and the meetings at Evanston, Illinois, in 1954 and New Delhi, India, in 1961.

The Catholic Church, for its part, has always been interested in unity, regarding her oneness as an essential part of her divine origin. As Catholics, we believe that our unity has never been lost and that the Church Christ founded can never lose its unity. Our interest in the cause of Christian union is, for love of God, to bring back into the unity of the Church those who have lost that unity.

We do not say this in a false sense of superiority; instead, we hold this truth in all humility, well aware of the great obligations it places on us—the possessors of the truth and unity of Christ—to share that truth and unity with those who are so earnestly seeking it. Our unity is not a weapon to be used against those who do not share it; rather it is a responsibility to extend it.

Christian unity was certainly frequently on the mind of Pope Pius XII. He spoke often of this problem and on various occasions issued invitations to all Christians to return to the unity of Holy Mother Church. He also took up in his historic 1953 address to the Italian jurists the problem of religious tolerance in modern society. Further, during his reign there was issued an Instruction by the Sacred Congregation of the Holy Office, which is regarded as the Magna Charta of the Catholic ecumenical movement by many historians of this movement.

The Instruction exhorted bishops "to make a special object of their care and attention this work of 'reunion' which is a particular charge and duty of the Church. They must not only use great diligence in keeping all this under effective supervision, but give it prudent encouragement and direction with the twofold purpose of assisting those who are in search of truth and the true Church and of shielding the faithful from the dangers which so easily accompany the progress of this movement." Although a note of caution is sounded, the general tone of the Instruction is one of great encouragement for Catholics to participate in the work of Christian unity.

For all practical purposes, the Catholic layman in America, even the well-instructed one, has little immediate personal interest in the official dialogue carried on by theologians. He does, however, have a most crucial role to play in what we might call the "unofficial dialogue." One reason he is important was explained by an outstanding American Catholic ecumenical leader, Father John Sheerin, C.S.P., editor of *Catholic World,* who asserted in an editorial (March, 1961):

"It seems to me that the Protestants in America are not yet ready to sit down to strictly theological discussions. Our ultimate differences are theological but we have to clear away a mass of political, social and historical misconceptions and misunderstandings before we can hope to get down to the theological questions. Free bus transportation, federal aid to parochial schools, the Legion of Decency are issues that command more Protestant attention and cause more religious friction than doctrines such as Redemption and Justification. Until we have competent lay Catholics to represent the Catholic point of view on these questions I don't see how we can expect any fruits from top-level dialogue."

It is both highly desirable and essential that the theologians from the various faiths meet and discuss the theological causes of disunity and unity. For ultimately, of course, our problems are primarily those of theological disunity. But over the centuries so many social, political, and cultural weeds have grown in the garden of unity that a lot of weeding out of side issues and false attitudes on both sides is going to have to take place before the flowers of theological unity are going to begin to grow. And as much of this weeding-out process is going to have to be carried out by lay people as by theologians.

This is hard work, frequently slow-going and often disappointing. As a result, many Catholics tend to take a negative attitude toward the whole process, putting the burden of seeking reunion on the shoulders of non-Catholics. Their feelings become particularly violent every time an irresponsible or uninformed non-Catholic issues a statement filled with canards about the Church.

Yet, despite all the justifiable righteousness on our side, it cannot be denied that we carry a heavy burden of responsibility to initiate and sustain ventures or relationships in the cause of unity. In his excellent little *Protestant Hopes and the Catholic Responsibility*, ecumenical expert Father George Tavard explains:

"The real problem of Catholic responsibility concerns us today. After listening to the lessons of the past we should correct our behavior where correction is required. For we ourselves constitute an obstacle to the reunion of Christendom insofar as we are not Catholic enough. By this I do not mean 'holy' enough. The question is not one of personal virtue. Prayer and fasting are alone able to drive some demons away, and the demon of Christian disunion may well be one of these. . . . This, however, is a matter for the unexpected grace of God. The Spirit may so move a soul if he wants; but we know nothing about it. As regards the Catholic community in general, the problem is not one of personal virtue, but of collective behavior. Non-Catholics do not judge the Church by her collective behavior. Non-Catholics do not judge the Church by her spiritual elite. They no doubt suspect that such an elite exists; but it does not strike their eyes every day. They accordingly judge the Church by averages, exactly as we judge non-Catholics. These averages cannot be scientifically established by a cursory survey. They can nevertheless be approximated by looking at ordinary parishes and reading ordinary Catholic weeklies. These are geared to averages and give a fairly good idea of what the Catholic average is. The problem is therefore to know if and why the average Catholic life presents an obstacle to Christian reunion."

We are faced, then, with the matter of what some persons have described as the "image" of the Church. It is up to each of us in our daily life to present a clear and attractive picture of the Church, the Mystical Body, worshiping God, loving our neighbor, working for the presence of justice, grace, and charity in the world, being present where Christ would want us to be, for His sake. In other words, living a life with as little of our smallness and imperfection in it as possible and as much as we can demonstrating the vitality and charity of Christ and His Church.

But, today, what do non-Catholics see? How does the image of the Church look to them? A Catholic, Dr. George N. Shuster, president of Hunter College for twenty years, wrote in *Ave Maria*, that to the non-Catholic the image of the Church "is still one of the exclusiveness of the Catholic. Here nothing has changed fundamentally. The Church is a series of fences from behind which he is not permitted to come. He must be born, married, educated, buried by himself. And, of course, the major objective is to get enough people inside the fences so that at a given moment they can jump out and overwhelm everybody else. The better educated, in the modern sense, the outsider is, the surer he feels that the reason for the fences is sheer obscurantism. In the market of ideas Catholic wares would in his view be difficult to sell. There exists a widespread good will toward the Catholics one meets in business, in politics or at cocktail parties. There is very, very little in the whole realm of the intelligence."

Much the same thing was said by a Presbyterian minister, Robert McAfee Brown, at the invitation of a Catholic publisher who asked some Protestants and Jews for their image of the Church today. Rev. Brown pointed out in the resulting book, *American Catholics, A Protestant-Jewish View*, that many non-Catholics see Catholicism as "a kind of monolithic structure. In its crudest form, this image of the Church suggests that the hierarchy has a uniform opinion on absolutely everything and that the laity believe and do whatever the hierarchy tells them to believe and do about absolutely everything. Every Catholic is part of this structure, usually called a 'power structure,' and will in no way deviate from what he is told to do."

To correct false images, to project the true image of the Church is one of the most insistent challenges demanding the attention of the contemporary Catholic layman. Not only is this challenge and opportunity his because of the obligations explained by Father Tavard; it is also his because of the plain and obvious fact that the nation in which we live is a Protestant nation in quantity and in custom. Because we are *American* Catholics, we must deal with Protestants whatever our personal preference—although in an irenic mood we can certainly hope that the preferences of Catholics would be positive.

To go effectively about our work of correcting false images, we need some basic understanding of how Protestants regard us—and why. As well as how and why non-Catholics approach the ecumenical round table. For example, it has been pointed out that earlier this century Protestant ecumenical activity, influenced by Anglican thinking, was somewhat of an intellectual approach concerned with doctrinal content; this was the so-called faith and order movement. But reductionism, fostered by the multiplicity of sects and denominations, brought about a shift to the life and work movement, which glossed over doctrinal problems and intellectualism and instead rested on the work being performed by religious groups. What has been called intellectual ecumenism is now something of a dead issue in terms of a widespread popular movement. The emphasis instead is on "spiritual ecumenics," in which we and others pray for greater "spiritual maturity" for all religious people and groups.

To make my point more specific, I recall giving a private talk to a group of ministers and rabbis just before the presidential election of 1960 on the Catholic view of Church-state relations. I developed the theory of Church-state relations as seen by Catholics historically, along with some contemporary

comments from authoritative sources. During the question
and answer period which followed, there were virtually no
questions on the theory of the subject. Instead, almost every
question was something like: "I was a missionary in Latin
America for two years and the Catholic country I was in
treated us Protestants badly." Or, "Why aren't there Protestants on the police force in ——— (an adjoining city)?" Or,
"Catholics don't seem to be interested in our most democratic
institution, our public school system."

When the session was over, a rabbi present was asked to
summarize the meeting. In so doing, he made an excellent
point, putting his finger immediately on the different manner
in which Protestant and Catholic minds work within an ecumenical framework. He asserted that the Catholic mind tended
to think in terms of the theory that showed nothing incompatible between the Church's teachings and democracy. But
the Protestant mind was existential; it thought in terms of concrete situations that existed, regardless of what the theory
said.

In practice, I believe this means we American Catholics—
the Church—are going to be judged (the image of the Church
is going to be projected) primarily on our responsible actions
for freedom in the community and not on how well we know
the theory of the Church on the relations between the Church
and the state. Our words will be important, but not nearly so
important in every area of our lives as our daily deeds in our
neighborhood, our city, our nation.

The first step which every Catholic layman can and must
take in his dealings with his non-Catholic brothers is to develop a sense of love for those who err, though rejecting the
error. Cardinal Augustin Bea, S.J., chairman of the Ecumenical Council's Secretariat for Promoting Christian Unity, put it
this way in an address:

"This means, therefore, jealous care of our personal salvation in Faith, an unshakeable determination always to protect
the complete integrity of Catholic dogma, and love for those
who err, meeting them with the greatest possible understand-

ing, without resentments of prejudices and with real and effective Christian charity."

In our daily lives, this means most of all that our whole attitude toward non-Catholics be one of love and respect for their humanity with a willingness to demonstrate our good will whenever the occasion requires it. In sum, for love of Christ we love all men, for whom He suffered and died on the Cross. At this point, however, a danger arises.

This danger occurred to me on an occasion when I was attending a dialogue meeting with public and private seminars with Catholic, Protestant, and Jewish clergy and laymen and a Greek Orthodox priest. The entire affair was a happy and fruitful one with a great deal of Christian charity exhibited on all sides. The men and women involved were people of personal charm and friendliness who would not want to hurt anyone's feelings by sharp public disagreement.

This kind of atmosphere is quite common among groups being introduced to the ecumenical encounter for the first time. The good, religious people involved find out to their mutual surprise that they have more in common than they originally thought. The situation is so pleasant that it encourages a kind of honeymoon period, which, not unlike marriage, has to come to a halt sometime.

Now in ecumenics as in marriage, a honeymoon is a splendid idea. But in neither case can you live on love alone. You simply have to come to grips with reality. And in the case of the reunion of Christians we must face up to the fact sooner or later that there are serious differences of opinion and doctrine dividing us. Indeed, we hardly understand each other's thinking even in basic approaches to religion.

But, having begun our quest in a spirit of love and having made some contacts with non-Catholics, what can we do to make these contacts more fruitful and permanent? This brings us to our second step—that of more prolonged and permanent contact with non-Catholics—which we can pursue on both informal and more formal, official levels.

On the informal level, beginnings are being made quietly

and effectively in many parts of the country, although there is certainly no mass movement underway by any means. But typical of the groups pioneering this kind of informal, getting-to-know-you-better meeting is one in Tulsa, Oklahoma, which meets monthly. The group includes Presbyterian, Unitarian, Catholic, and National Baptist laymen; Episcopal and Methodist laywomen; a Missouri Synod Lutheran pastor; a rabbi of the reformed Jewish tradition and several Catholic priests.

The group is not trying particularly to accomplish anything in a formal sense. Their main interest is becoming acquainted with each other's beliefs better. The group makes it possible for them to meet in a friendly, relaxed atmosphere in which they can be honest with each other without having to worry about making points or winning arguments.

At the other end of the country, John B. Mannion, executive secretary of the National Liturgical Conference in Washington, D.C., described the group with which he is engaged in *Catholic World*. The group, which meets almost every month, consists of five Episcopalians (including their priest or his wife), three or four Lutherans (often including their pastor), one or two Methodists (also with their minister), and three or four Catholics, usually including a priest. The members get together at each other's homes and have dealt with such questions as What is the Church?, the Bible, sin, salvation, prayer, public worship, confession, indulgences, devotion to the saints, and similar matters. As Mr. Mannion notes, these are not formal or official discussions, but rather ones aimed at clarifying and understanding each other's beliefs rather than attempting to resolve the differences.

And from these meetings, Mr. Mannion has detected three results in the lives of the members of the group. First, they have a more profound sense of the tragedy that is disunion. Second, they have actually achieved a better understanding of each other's beliefs and can see the points of unity that exist. Finally, they have grown personally as Christians by having had to learn more about their respective faiths and to distinguish between the essential and the nonessential.

These are typical of two kinds of informal groups. There is also a need for more formal, official groups.

I do not mean formal or official in the sense of theological meetings, but rather only in terms of meeting on a broader community basis dealing with public problems. It should be noted that there are virtually no such groups actually in existence today, although there certainly are related groups—such as human relations commissions in various cities; more often than not, however, these are concerned mostly with the problems of minority groups and race relations.

But we greatly need today more groups of Protestants, Catholics, and Jews who will meet to discuss and attempt to arrive at some solutions for religious tensions and conflicts which have manifested themselves *on the civic level.*

I am thinking particularly of problems such as prayer in the public schools, Sunday closing laws, aid to education, and many such related problems. The purpose of such groups would be to meet to discuss ways and means by which civic problems with religious overtones can be effectively dealt with, without creating unnecessary religious conflicts. Although it may on occasion be desirable, it would certainly not be necessary for these groups to have any official status or have any official representatives from the various religious groups represented within the community.

The groups would not exist primarily to arrive at official solutions. Their purpose, instead, would be to make available a kind of structure through which such problems could be discussed and for which solutions might possibly be found on the civic level without involving the official religious groups themselves. Had such groups existed, for example, during the acrid, frequently bitter and often confused federal aid to education debate of 1961 it is quite possible that a great deal of the religious tension which eventually developed might never have got off the ground.

It is a fact that the various religious groups usually have no channels through which they can deal with each other formally or informally. Catholics, Protestants, and Jews all have their own official organizational structures existing in a kind of parallel series alongside each other but never crossing. When an issue develops—often suddenly and unexpectedly—within a community each religious group often issues its own statements and initiates its own publicity. Take the case of federal aid to education or the Sunday closing laws. Each church group issues an official statement of one kind or another, but the laymen who are vitally affected both as citizens and as religious adherents have no structure through which their voice can be heard.

It seems to me that it is important for them to meet within the framework of some kind of civic or political structure in which, officially as citizens, unofficially as members of their respective churches, they can discuss the civic and political aspects of the particular problem at issue and attempt to work out some solutions which could at least be seriously considered and possibly even acted upon both by the religious groups and local governments affected. Such groups may or may not be effective in every case—but at least by their very existence they offer a hope for solutions that can never be reached if such organizations never come into existence.

And at the same time such groups offer, as a side benefit, unlimited ecumenical opportunities, drawing together as they would many of the better representatives of the various religious groups that are to be found in a particular community.

These are some of the forms of official and unofficial, formal and informal, civic and private dialogue and confrontation which can be acted upon and developed by the Catholic laymen in America in cooperation with non-Catholics of good will. There is room for direct discussions of religion or for a more indirect approach through cooperation in the civic community. (As Bishop John J. Wright of Pittsburgh noted in an address to a meeting on Christian unity at Maynooth, Ireland, in 1961: "Above all, if there cannot be immediate unity of faith, there must be unity of love, expressing itself in common effort in social, economic and political relations.")

But regardless of what form the attempts at more understanding and the formation of a deeply rooted spirit of good will might take, there are some ground rules for the dialogue, which must be followed and which have proved their worth often in practice. The rules were spelled out in detail by Robert McAfee Brown in "Rules for the Dialogue," which was published simultaneously in *The Commonweal* and the *Christian Century* in 1960. Summarized briefly, here are the rules:

1. Each partner in the dialogue must believe that the other is speaking in good faith. There must be a common devotion to the One Who said "I am the . . . truth."

2. Each partner must have a clear understanding of his own faith. This is obviously more of a problem for Protestants whose beliefs cannot be formulated in a precise manner as can those of Catholics.

3. Each partner must strive for a clear understanding of the faith of the other. This is both a precondition and a result of the dialogue. There are two important corollaries to this point:

    a. A willingness to interpret the faith of the other in its best light rather than its worst.

    b. Each partner must maintain a continual willingness to revise his understanding of the faith of the other.

4. Each partner must accept responsibility in humility and penitence for what his group has done and is doing to foster and perpetuate division.

5. Each partner must forthrightly face the issues which cause separation, as well as those which create unity. We must face the fact that real differences do exist and so sometimes do real sources of unity.

6. The final and most important rule is this: Each partner must recognize that all that can be done with the dialogue is to offer it up to God. We must be willing to do our best and then leave the results up to the workings of God.

Whatever form of the apostolate of Christian unity we follow as laymen in America, according to our talents and special abilities and preferences, there can at least be no question about the fact that we must make every effort to do *something*. The scandal of disunity is a burden that must be borne by each of us, uneasily and with a consuming desire to relieve it.

The operation of the Holy Spirit apart, the future of the ecumenical movement and the relief of religious tensions between Catholics and non-Catholics in America is going to depend to a significant degree on how well laymen recognize and accept the fact that they indeed have a crucial role to play in the unofficial dialogue. If laymen will become aware of and act on their obligations and responsibilities in this area, we can look forward with renewed hope and confidence toward the day when there will be "one fold and one Shepherd" (John 10:16).

CHAPTER 14

Catholics and Controversy

As a group, American Catholics either tend to shun controversy or when they do engage in it they all too often choose the wrong issues to debate. Unfortunately, their failures and inadequacies are proving harmful to the progress of the Church in the United States.

Another way of saying this is to point out that the Church is often not defended at all or that she is not infrequently represented badly by well-meaning but incompetent defenders. Further, many times the Church's impromptu champions select impossible positions and then proceed to fight to hold them with all the ardor of their irrational hearts.

Some Catholics, for example, indiscriminately justify the actions of all the Church's personnel and institutions, thus often doing more harm than good in the mind of the rational critic who may be looking more for information than for polemics. In the minds of some Catholics, to criticize the political or social views of a cleric, to disagree with a particular Church ruling not connected with faith or morals, or to question the techniques of a Catholic educational institution is akin to waving the traditional red flag in front of an infuriated bull. And the rationality of the two at that moment is often at about the same level.

But as a rule our problem is not that of the overzealous defender of the Church; it is, rather, that there is a puzzling lack of guardians of any stripe. I say puzzling because many Catholics who have distinguished themselves for their rhetorical competence in civic or political or professional life often become strangely silent when the subject of religion is up for discussion. Some probably are merely following the old American custom of not discussing religion. Others undoubtedly feel ill at ease and unprepared in a field usually presided over by the clergy.

And this is a most salient point to remember in terms of the lay apostolate and the role of the layman in American society today: So long as the layman does not tend to regard himself as the Church, but instead thinks of himself as belonging to the Church (owned and operated by the professional clergy), he will not naturally tend to defend the Church (himself) simply because he will not think of himself as being attacked.

Yet, if we don't begin to develop this attitude of being the Church in ourself and in others, we are failing Christ in the world. He has, after all, willed to carry on His mission in time through the Church, the clergy and laity alike. Our functions may differ, but we share the most important long-range goals. If Christ is to find a place in our world we must help make that place, we must help form a public opinion that will be conducive to the spiritual and temporal good of men. And one of the most important ways by which a public opinion is formed is through the processes of public and private controversy and discussion.

It is paramount for us as Catholics and citizens to understand the meaning and role of both public opinion and controversy.

"Public opinion," said Pope Pius XII in an address in 1950 to a convention of Catholic journalists, "is the mark of every normal society composed of men who, conscious of their personal and social conduct, are intimately concerned with the community to which they belong. When all is said and done, public opinion is everywhere the natural echo, the common resounding, more or less spontaneously, of events and the present situation in man's mind and judgment. Where public opinion fails to manifest itself, where it does not exist at all—whatever the reasons for its silence or absence—one must see in this lack something vicious, a malady, a disease of social life."

The pope then made some very pertinent remarks about the role of the press in public opinion, a role which is served as well by the Catholic controversialists in or out of the press.

The press controversialist, said Pope Pius, "has an eminent role to play in the formation of opinion, not by dictating or regimenting it, but by serving it usefully. . . . Catholic journalists will always refrain from 'making' opinion. Better, they will aspire to serve it."

And we can serve the formation of a healthy public opinion by the medium of controversy, discussion, and debate. This is not controversy for its own sake; rather it is a discussion of issues aimed at seeing that all sides are heard so that public opinion will be served, not "made." Controversy, then, is not quarreling over the back fence. It is, at its best, the presentation of *the* Catholic view in matters involving faith and morals in which there is such a view or it may well be the presentation of *a* Catholic view, a view consistent with the Church's teachings on a matter in which there is no single official view. And controversy may take place within the Church itself or between the Church or individual Christians and the temporal order.

Within the Church there is plenty of room for differences of opinion and varied views and as within any other social unit a public opinion should be encouraged here. In his 1950 address, Pope Pius noted that, "because the Church is a living body, something would be wanting in her life if public opinion were lacking—and the blame for this deficiency would fall back upon the pastors and the faithful. Here again the Catholic press [read controversialist] can render useful service. To this service, however, more than to any other, the journalist must bring that character of which We have spoken. This character consists of unalterable respect and deep love toward the Divine order; that is to say, in the present case toward the Church as she exists, not only in the eternal designs but as she actually lives here below in space and time—Divine yes, but formed by human limbs and organs.

"If he possesses this character, the Catholic writer will

know how to guard himself against mute servility as well as against uncontrolled criticism. With a firm clarity he will contribute toward the formation of a Catholic opinion within the Church, above all when, as is the case today, this opinion vacillates between an illusory and unreal spirituality and a defeatist and materialistic realism."

Pope Pius developed these ideas further in a message to the 1957 meeting of the Catholic Press Association of the United States and Canada, meeting in St. Louis. Pointing out the need of obedience and devotion to Christ and His Bishops, he continued:

"But in regard to questions in which the divinely appointed teachers have not pronounced judgment—and the field is vast and varied, saving that of faith and morals—free discussion will be altogether legitimate, and each one may hold and defend his own opinion. But let such an opinion be presented with due restraint; and no one will condemn another simply because he does not agree with his opinion, much less challenge his loyalty."

Thus it is easily seen that there is plenty of room for the serving of public opinion within the Church and in an earlier chapter we considered some of the areas in which this was especially true. But in many ways the most immediately pressing need for laymen is to take a more active and vital part in the formation and service of public opinion within the community in this year of Our Lord. For the Church has been badly hurt in our times precisely because of our failure to engage in controversy in the community.

One of the most recent instances of the harm done to the Church by the inaction of the laity was the federal aid-to-education fight in 1961. By their failure to speak up and out, lay people contributed toward the formation of a false image—a false public opinion—of the Church, which will continue to hurt us for years and years ahead.

During the controversy a significant number of Catholic parents were playing an important role in working for an aid-to-education bill that would assist their children in private schools. These individuals, alone and in groups, were not acting as Catholics; they were acting primarily as citizens for what they regarded as justice for their children. And it is most important to note that many of them did not agree with the position taken publicly by some members of the clergy that loans to private schools would be desirable; in point of fact many of these parents regarded loans as an insult. As one of them said to me, "If Congress thinks it is going to lend me back my own money—at interest—I think it time the House and Senate be given a rude awakening."

The point is, however, that despite this swelling opinion and action on the part of many Catholic citizens, the communications media gave the impression it was the "official" Church leading the fight. Catholic parents' groups received little or no attention; the play was given by secular news organs to statements by the bishops; in various national TV debates the "Catholic position" was presented by priests—as if there were only one acceptable Catholic view on the whole matter.

The non-Catholic on the outside looking in could hardly be blamed if he formed the opinion that in this matter Catholics were tools of the clergy and were being whipped into line by the bishops and priests. One of the major reasons for this state of affairs was, of course, our failure as laymen to take part in the service and formation of public opinion through controversy. We are so accustomed to letting the clergy speak for us or of having no voice that we got caught in the trap of our own inactivity. The truth was that Catholics were split on the issue. Some wanted no aid at all either for Catholic or public schools. Others were for federal aid, but wanted it to include Catholic children also. Some regarded construction loans as acceptable; others were dead set against them. But little of this division among Catholics ever got across to our fellow citizens. All our non-Catholic friends saw or heard was an "official line" that developed by default, simply because there weren't enough Catholic laymen making their voices heard on all sides of the controverted issue.

Another opportunity missed here was the chance to explain the differences between *a* Catholic viewpoint and *the* Catholic viewpoint. Even though Catholics all shared *the* Catholic view on the *principles* involved in the discussion, there was plenty of room for division of opinion on the *application* of these principles to the specific problem of federal aid in the year of 1961 in the United States under certain conditions.

As Archbishop Karl J. Alter, chairman of the Administrative Board of the National Catholic Welfare Conference, said at the time: "The question of whether or not there ought to be federal aid is a judgment to be based on objective economic facts connected with the schools of the country, and consequently Catholics are free to take a position in accordance with these facts."

Catholics were not free, though, in the principles involved: That is, they were obliged to work for a law that would achieve the common good or come as close to it as possible. The differences of opinion arose over what the common good was in 1961. Some Catholics wanted to see the Administration's no-aid-to-private-schools bill passed because they feared that if the bill were scuttled this would cause anti-Catholic feeling; thus, for them, the passage of the bill was the best way to achieve the common good. Other Catholics held the position that no bill would be better than what they regarded as a bad bill that would perpetuate what they regarded as injustice. And still others opposed the bill purely on political and economic grounds, believing the local community should pay the education bill locally. Others yet feared that once the federal government became involved it would attempt to dominate the curriculum of the private schools.

In point of fact, however, there was no strictly official Catholic view on the matter which Catholics had to hold in order to remain in good standing with the Church. And because Catholic laymen failed to take part vigorously and intelligently in the entire matter a false image of the Church arose giving the lie to the very principle which makes the Church—on the human level—desirable and tenable for a free man: a respect for freedom of conscience.

In the first place, then, the Catholic layman should not only have a firm grasp of what the Church's position is or is not on controverted issues, he should also know the difference between *the* Catholic viewpoint and *a* Catholic viewpoint.

Secondly, he must have an understanding of the non-Catholic mind in practice. In the preceding chapter I used the example of the rabbi who summarized a talk I gave to some Protestant ministers on Church-state relations and the discussion that followed. He pointed out that the Catholic mind tended to think in terms of the theory which showed nothing incompatible between the Church's teachings and democracy, but the Protestant mind was existential, it thought in terms of concrete situations that existed, irrespective of what the theory said.

This puts a special obligation on us to make our actions in the community crystal clear whenever there is any danger of being misinterpreted. Are we, for instance, in favor of equal federal aid to parochial schools as well as public schools? We should make every effort to see that our position is projected accurately: We are arguing from a position of justice, for our equal rights and those of our children; this is no secret or hidden maneuver to subvert the public school system or to secure government support for our religion. We should be willing to take the initiative and walk that extra mile to make our motives and views known. The extra effort we put into demonstrating our willingness to meet openly with non-Catholics (or Catholics) who may disagree with our views will not only help clarify our position but it might well win some converts to the justice of our cause as well.

Another thorny issue is that of the birth control laws. The Church is unequivocally opposed to the use of contraceptives, but a strong case may be made as to why Catholics should *not* vote to put or keep on the books laws forbidding the use of contraceptives. For one thing, such a law is virtually unenforceable, requiring, as it has been said, a policeman in every bedroom. And applying the principles of Pius XII and Cardinal Lercaro, Catholics may easily arrive at the conclusion that a greater good may be obtained by keeping such laws from being passed or kept in force. There is no single Catholic position on such an issue, requiring as it does many prudential judgments; but whatever views Catholics take it would be most desirable for them to make the reasons for them clear and understandable.

I think the steps that can and should be taken in particular community situations will become clear for the Catholics involved in each special instance. What is important to remember is that the Church and the cause of religious tolerance both have much to gain by a friendly attitude that demonstrates willingness to discuss both sides of each issue. If we do not we may easily give our non-Catholic friends the impression that we are quick to issue statements in favor of religious freedom but reluctant to put them into practice.

This brings up a third point, namely, that controversy need not be belligerent or unfriendly. Over the years some of my friendliest opponents have been ministers and Jewish lay people; to the best of my knowledge none of us has given an inch in our religious principles, but we have—through our discussions and controversies—through our presentation of opposing views—managed sometimes on the civic level, as citizens, to reconcile our views for the sake of the common good.

And this, after all, is the fruit of controversy—to be able to resolve problems. In some circumstances it is possible and even likely that a particular controversy may continue to rage for untold years with us continually called upon to state and restate our views with little or no hope of any resolution of the matter. Yet, our goal must always be the resolution of controverted issues, not their prolongation. And our discussions must always be carried on in the spirit of Christ.

A fourth point in regard to controversy involves "imposing our views." This is a problem so complicated that it deserves and undoubtedly one day will have a book written about it;

yet, since it comes up constantly during the course of public debate it is well for the Catholic controversialist to be fore-warned.

In the case of birth control, where the Catholic may be speaking as a Catholic—that is, presenting the Church's views on the use of artificial contraceptives—or in the matter of, say, federal aid in which a Catholic citizen takes the view that his children are being discriminated against, in either case, at one time or another the Catholic controversialist is going to be told that he is trying to "impose his views" on his fellow citizens.

I once engaged in a controversy with a writer for a well-known secular journal of opinion over the matter of birth control. It was her view that "the Church" was trying to "impose" its views, its own particular concept of morality on her. She was in favor of artificial birth control and felt strongly that it should be made part of our foreign aid program. She was upset that certain religious groups were blocking this approach.

Part of the burden of my argument was to point out that I really felt that I was the offended party. After all, she was trying to impose *her* view of morality on *me*. And in the give and take of democracy every group tries to "impose" its views of one kind or another on the rest of the country. The significant point is that we must not "impose" our views in such a way as to limit unreasonably the freedom of thought or action of our fellow citizens. We are constantly in a monumental struggle of competing and often conflicting moral opinions, each seeking to align and reinforce itself with political power. Our goal is to find a way out that will neither compromise principle nor lead to complete inaction and ineffectiveness on both sides.

I do not believe Catholic controversialists should fear the label of wanting to "impose their views." I do feel, however, that they should exercise the greatest caution so in practice they do not infringe on the rights and consciences of their fellow Americans. Labels can only be harmful when they cor-respond to reality. If we show, despite our vigorous and dedicated support of our position, that we are also concerned about the civil rights of others, the labels will not stick.

Finally, I believe the cause of an effective and robust Catholic controversy will best be served by laity and clergy working together to help each other do his job. The laity particularly have a job to do here, which they have too often neglected in the past.

This is well illustrated by Father Robert McDole of Oklahoma City. He was arrested in 1961 for participating in a sit-in demonstration with Negro students. And he was bodily carted off to jail a second time for repeating his action.

Laymen might ponder the words of Bishop Victor J. Reed of Oklahoma City on the occasion of Father's first arrest:

"It is the duty of the clergy to preach, to teach, and to form the consciences of the laity with respect to the civic and social implications of Christ's teachings on the dignity and equality of men. It is primarily the responsibility of the laity to see that these teachings are translated into our civic and social relations. In isolated and exceptional instances—and in the absence of sufficient lay activity—the clergy may take direct action in these matters.

"The question of propriety in the situation before us—a priest taking part in a demonstration which I would say is ordinarily the forum of the laity—is a matter on which there can be differences of opinion. I am inclined to think that the present situation justifies Father McDole's action."

Laymen can hardly complain about the image of the Church being distorted and misunderstood in the public forum when they are so reluctant to take part in the controversy and present the Church's views or the views of responsible Christians. We have so let our work be done by the clergy that we are harming the Church by our failures. We have become so timid to think and act responsibly as respectable laymen that we have done a great disservice to the Church and especially to the clergy. How? Read these words of Jesuit Father Yves de Montcheuil in his *For Men of Action:*

"While the laity should ask the clergy for light on the doctrine of the Church, they should avoid submitting to a decision of the ecclesiastical hierarchy if that decision really belongs to the laity. If the faithful do not have the courage to assume their responsibilities and if they develop the habit of trying to cover themselves unnecessarily with a decision of authority, there is the danger of giving the clergy the unfortunate habit of intervening too much in the choice of temporal institutions. After that, one would be out of order in complaining of a clericalism which he has provoked and which is practically made necessary by his own pusillanimity. On the other hand, no one should begrudge the layman that territory which is reserved for him, or reproach him for performing himself the work which is entrusted to him. The laity should be instructed, formed, checked on, and judged, but not bridled or hindered."

And Father de Montcheuil wisely notes: "By accepting their responsibilities, the laity will cease to provoke the clergy to intervene in a domain where they have no business."

In the years ahead of us, the future of the Church will depend on many interrelated factors. But it is not too much to say that one of the most vital of those elements is going to be how generously laymen respond to the need the Church has of their services as controversialists. And this will depend in no small part on how wisely and well the clergy and laity come to know and understand each other's position in our American democracy and by how well laymen perform the duties which are distinctively theirs.

Unless laymen contribute their share to the cause of the formation and service of public opinion within the Church and the community great harm will be incurred in both the City of God and of Man. In Pius XII's words in his 1950 address: "In truth, where public opinion ceases to function freely, there peace is in peril."

CHAPTER 15

Conservatives, Liberals, and Catholicism

"May a Catholic be a conservative anymore?" is a question that was asked, sometimes seriously, after Pope John XXIII's great social encyclical on *Christianity and Social Progress* was published in 1961. When I read it at that time in the question and answer column of a diocesan newspaper, I thought immediately of the first time the question had been put to me—over a decade before, when I was teaching a course in the papal social encyclicals at a Catholic university. The question is an old one and will, I am sure, be asked again and again in the future.

When it is asked seriously, the occasion is often when a previously uninstructed Catholic suddenly becomes aware of the vast and far-reaching social doctrines of the Church. For the first time he sometimes sees how what are often regarded as "conservative" positions have been repudiated by the Church's social teachings. The result is confusion and the student—whatever his age—asks his inevitable question.

Before attempting to ask that question, however, it is helpful to have some basic grasp of what is meant by the terms conservative and liberal.

In practice, we must begin by distinguishing among at least economic, political, and religious liberalism and conservatism. Take liberalism, for instance. It is quite possible for people to disbelieve in *religious* liberalism and still be able to hold, for example, *economic* liberalism; not a few American Catholics display this combination. Similarly, it is not infrequent for people to believe in religious liberalism and to disbelieve in economic liberalism. Thus, many Protestants who are very critical of the existing economic system are at the same time believers in complete religious freedom without benefit of creed, code, or cult.

These preliminary considerations give us some hint of what is meant by the various forms of liberalism or individualism. Religious liberalism emphasizes personal religious autonomy and freedom from the authority of *institutionalized religion*. At the time of the Protestant Revolution, many of the Protestant leaders were examples of that; today, within the existing Protestant framework there are both sects which tend to de-emphasize doctrine and an institutional framework as well as the more conservative elements which stress a creed and a strong, organized Church.

Political liberalism, or individualism, was a movement directed toward freedom for the individual against the government; it was a reaction against government red tape, against mercantilism, against despotism. As Bishop George Beck, A.A., has pointed out in *Catholic Mind*: ". . . the name 'Liberal' was first used in Spain in the 1820s in opposition to the word 'servile' and was intended to denote the party which stood for constitutional and national freedom."

The social doctrine of the Church, however, is most interested in *economic liberalism*, understood especially as a theory which holds that the *sole* regulating principle of economic life is the free activity of the market place. Other names for this idea are economic individualism, liberal capitalism, the Manchester school of economics, and *laissez faire*. In terms of American usage, individualism might be the best term to use, since probably more people understand this. But the encyclicals generally use the term "liberalism."

It should be immediately clear that a distinction is necessary between the American use of the term liberal and the European or classical use of the term. Although we shall examine this more closely, when we think of liberals or liberalism in the United States we usually think of political liberals, of "New Deal" or "Fair Deal" liberals who want a more liberal interpretation of the Constitution by the Supreme Court, who stand for civil rights, for international organization, and the like.

This is not what the encyclicals are talking about when they condemn liberalism. They are condemning, rather, economic liberalism—not political liberalism as we know it in the United States. The American equivalent of the social encyclicals' use of the term liberalism would be the "rugged individualism" which was so praised before the Great Depression of 1929. For purposes of clarity, therefore, it is essential for us to keep all these distinctions in mind.

There is no question, then, that the Church's social teaching has condemned classical economic liberalism. And certainly there is no doubt where the Church stands on religious liberalism. But what about political liberalism?

First, perhaps, we should allow the conservatives and the liberals to speak for themselves, to attempt to define or describe their own positions. Author and educator Russell Kirk, for instance, has in *The Intelligent Woman's Guide to Conservatism* defined a conservative as "a person who endeavors to conserve the best in our traditions and our institutions, reconciling the best with necessary reform from time to time."

On the occasion of its thirty-fifth anniversary in 1959 the editors of *Commonweal*, a magazine edited by Catholic laymen, engaged in some soul-searching about their beliefs and commented that ". . . the editors of this magazine clearly tend to be 'liberal,' not in the nineteenth century European sense but in the modern American sense of the word. We are deeply committed to the idea of political democracy, and we have little patience with Catholic writers who discuss political questions as if nothing had happened between the French Revolution and the present. We value the American Constitution and oppose any interference with due process of law. We cherish our own civil liberties, and we defend those of others. We abhor anti-Semitism or racial discrimination in any form. We are deeply concerned with genuine measures to fight Communism—moral, economic, military and psychological—and completely uninterested in 'anti-Communist crusades' that make bold headlines but signify nothing. We support domestic measures we think will help in achieving that social justice described in the papal social encyclicals, and we favor efforts to promote international social justice by aiding the under-developed nations. We think Catholics have not given enough thought to what it means to live in a pluralistic society and we consider it imperative that they repair this omission. These are some of the things we stand for, under whatever label they can be found. If doing so makes us liberal, we are liberal; these are good causes, no matter what name is put to them, and we will continue to support them in the years ahead."

If the amount of space given to the "liberal" description above seems greater than that given to the conservative, this is no coincidence. It is symptomatic of the fact that responsible Catholic conservatives simply are not numerically articulate in the enunciation of their views. They have, unfortunately, fallen into a situation somewhat analogous to that of some opposition congressmen and senators during the long reign of the Democrats during the 1930s and 1940s; they spent so much time being the opposition that they neglected the build-ing of a consensus of principles on which they could agree. For some reason, psychological, historical, or otherwise, the American Catholic conservative seems to have fallen into the same trap.

Whatever the reason, it can be demonstrated that Ameri-can Catholic conservatives simply have not devoted any no-ticeable amount of space in Catholic periodicals to the construction of a logical, tenable set of principles to guide and inspire them. For the past generation their unity and much of their motivation has come from their common opposition to communism and socialism; they have been sustained by what they have been against rather than by what they stood for. Verifying this is the experience of the Catholic newspaper editor regarded as more liberal than conservative. He wanted to run in his paper a conservative Catholic columnist for the sake of editorial balance. But it took him more than a year of searching before he could find one who was responsible, articu-late, and readable.

Another Catholic editor, Gerard E. Sherry, has made this

evaluation of the difference between liberals and conservatives. Every age, he notes, has its liberals and conservatives. But why does a man line up on one side or the other? Mr. Sherry answers:

"One factor which cannot be overlooked, or at least so it seems to me, is the basic emotional approach each man has to reality. Two men can stand before one and the same situation: One will be caught by the dangers involved and the other will be seized by the opportunities which it presents. Objectively the dangers and the opportunities have a constant value, but these two men place a greater emphasis on one over the other. Fundamentally the conservative is sensitive to dangers, and the liberal is sensitive to opportunities."

On the emotional level, Mr. Sherry's observations make a great deal of sense. But we must still search for an explanation of why all Catholics do not have the same approach to reality on a deeper and equally complex level, that of political judgment.

First, the responsible Catholic conservative and liberal can agree at least on the principles which unite them. Writing in *Commonweal* magazine on "the Conservative Catholic," an educator who is one, Frederick D. Wilhelmsen, confirms this when he says: "There can be no disagreement among Catholics about racism, segregation, trial by law as opposed to condemnation by innuendo, and analogous issues. There is only one possible Catholic principle on such things: the principle of justice."

For most rational, well-instructed Catholics there is no difficulty about the principles, but it is in the application of these principles that the Catholic conservative and liberal part company. Emotional predispositions aside, I believe the reason for the difference is primarily in the emphasis the individual wishes to put, based on his experience and judgment, on the *personal* or the *institutional* means to the end.

With some differences here and there, we can agree on the goals we wish to achieve. For example, Cardinal Amleto Cicognani, papal secretary of state, explained five points to be found in *Mater et Magistra* which he said were "neither very radical or very different" from the teachings of previous popes:

1) That working men should receive a wage sufficient to raise a family. 2) That forms of social security should be available everywhere. 3) That workers should have a voice in the running of the enterprise to which they devote their lives. 4) That workers ought likewise to have a more active voice in the councils that determine national economic policy. 5) That the wage contract ought to be modified by some form of partnership or some sharing in profits.

Assuming the acceptance of these goals as desirable and necessary by both Catholic conservatives and liberals, there would, I think, normally be two reactions: The liberal would likely point to Cardinal Cicognani's further statement on the same occasion in which he pointed out that the pope's emphasis on the "positive role of public authority" in *Mater et Magistra* is particularly pertinent because of the complexity of modern economic life. The liberal would also recall Pope John's approval of "socialization" and the intervention of the public authority as expressed in *Mater et Magistra*.

The conservative would point to Cardinal Cicognani's remark in the same interview on a visit to the United States in December, 1961, in which the cardinal noted that the pope "will not be misunderstood if due weight be given to the strong emphasis he throws on the primary role of the person, whether acting as an individual or within associations that respond to his natural social sense and buffer him against undue state intervention." And he would note Pope John's hearty approval of the principle of subsidiarity which, generally, limits state intervention to matters which cannot adequately be handled by lower governmental units.

So the end result would be two equally devout and well-instructed and loyal Catholics, both agreeing on at least five goals to be obtained, but differing on how they should be attained. The liberal probably would tend to stress that state intervention is needed to achieve many of the goals—e.g., social security—so he might suggest the idea of working on getting suitable legislation through the Congress to achieve these goals.

The conservative might well point out that there are dangers involved in turning to the state for help. That laws cannot change attitudes. That people can provide more for themselves than they think they can. That to deserve some form of partnership or sharing in profits workers should be forced to demonstrate a more responsible attitude toward the enterprises for which they work.

Can we say that either of these approaches is *the* Catholic way of achieving these goals? I do not think so. Both views have validity; both have things to be said in their favor. And both emphasize one or the other approach of the popes to the reconstruction of society.

The popes have said in their papal encyclicals that to construct a Christian society we must do two things: Reconstruct private and public morals. Reconstruct the institutions of society. In applying these to the political scene, one tends to be a personalist approach, emphasizing moral obligations and personal responsibility. The other tends to be social in its orientation and to rely more on changing the all-pervasive and penetrating influence of the social institution by social means, through legislation, or direct state action.

Neither approach has a monopoly on virtue. Both have much to recommend them in certain circumstances. Each is a respectable position worthy of attention and consideration. Although no individual holds to one position solely and without deviation, it may be said in general that the liberal tends to be an institutionalist, while the conservative tends to be a personalist. Basically, both the liberal and the conservative are deeply concerned over the attainment of human freedom in its various facets. Characteristically, however, the conservative tends to conserve this freedom by keeping authority at the lowest possible level, by not allowing the government to have too much authority over the lives of men. Paradoxically (or so it seems to some), liberalism combines the desire for individual freedom with a desire to achieve this freedom through the positive use of public authority.

Of course, this analysis does not by any means exhaust the possibilities for further discussion of the differences between conservatives and liberals. But it does show the validity of both approaches if used responsibly and not as a means to drag feet in the achievement of goals clearly defined on the level of principle in Catholic social teaching. Very often in practice there is no single "best" approach to many of our problems. Both a personal and an institutional approach may be needed to solve different aspects of the same problem.

And so we return to our question: May a Catholic be a conservative? The answer is that there is no answer. A conservative what? In the economic, religious, or political field?

Is the social doctrine of the Church liberal or conservative? If it is liberal, then we must be liberal; if it is conservative, then we must be likewise. In truth, however, it is neither. It is, rather, catholic and Catholic. It has elements of both the liberal and the conservative traditions. It has room for both the responsible liberal and the responsible conservative. What it asks first is dedication and devotion to the goals to be sought. It requires of both liberal and conservative that they study the social doctrine of the Church carefully and thoroughly to know what kind of society the Church wants us to have. What kind of society (or what possible *kinds* of societies) would be in keeping with Christian principles?

Perhaps most of all, however, within the context of the second half of the twentieth century, the social doctrine of the Church demands that we make every effort to work together, to respect and love each other with the love of Christ. Neither the conservative nor the liberal has a monopoly on truth. Instead of concentrating—as we have so often and so fruitlessly in the past—on the things that separate us, we might well devote our energies to a detailed consideration of the things that unite us. We have some urgent responsibilities in this field, as Pope John made quite clear in *Mater et Magistra*.

"In the application of this doctrine, however, there can

sometimes arise—even among sincere Catholics—differences of opinion. When this happens, they should be alert to preserve and give evidence of their mutual esteem and respect. At the same time, they should strive to find points of agreement for efficacious and suitable action. They should take special care, moreover, not to exhaust themselves in interminable discussions and, under pretext of seeking the better or the best, fail meanwhile to do the good that is possible and is thus obligatory."

Whatever our approach to the attainment of a Christian society—be we conservative or liberal—we share with our fellow members of the Mystical Body the rich and inexhaustible treasure of our social doctrine. Given the condition of the world which the American Catholic layman faces today, it is urgently incumbent that we give up the luxury of an indefinite sniping battle between the one approach or the other and begin to act responsibly by following Pope John's advice and making efforts to agree on the minimal "good that is possible and is thus obligatory."

I certainly do not mean that we should give up all public or private discussions and debates to arrive at a "united front." But we certainly must not restrict ourselves totally to theoretical discussions of the rightness or wrongness of each other's position. Let us add a new note—one of cooperation. What can we agree on? What plans of action can we share in specific cases so that our united strength might serve—if only in a limited way—to further the cause we all serve?

And in the socio-politico-economic order, that cause is the attainment of the common good, the general welfare of our community, our nation, our world. For though we may differ about our goals to some extent, and about the specific means to achieve them, the one great unifying factor which offers some hope of united action is the common good, the good of all. As Bishop John J. Wright wrote in *Catholic Mind* in a memorable manner:

"Such an appreciation of the 'common good,' which unites, as against—or, rather, as above—all particular or factional or partisan goods which divide, would make possible the 'vital center' which can exist only when honorable moderates of 'right' and 'left' prefer working with each other in behalf of the 'common good' to working with extremists of their own respective camps, extremists who seek only the particular good to which their side aspires. Thus, the present 'polarized' condition of society would be eased and social 'conservatives,' anxious to preserve the heritage out of the past, would have a common ground on which to meet and to work with social 'liberals' anxious to enlarge the hope of the future. The 'common good' includes, in the phrase of Scripture, *nova et vetera*—the old heritage and the new hopes.

"Thus, the conscientious citizen who walks a little left of center, freed from the embarrassment of constant association with senseless revolutionaries, should be able to make common cause in the quest for the common good with the no less honorable citizen who steers his course a little right of center and who is too often condemned as the friend of soulless reaction."

This is not an appeal for liberals or conservatives to give up their principles of thought and action to engage in a frenzied exchange of good will with the opposition. Nor is it an attempt to force an unreal unity on two irreconcilable philosophies. Reflecting the love of the Trinity, it is an effort by Catholic liberals and conservatives to search out elements of the general welfare on which they can find common ground and then work together for the achievement of goals precious to them both. It does not require them to put aside their debates or differences (for there shall always be some areas of real dispute).

It does mean, however, that we should be catholic and Catholic enough to rise above petty differences and overcome inconsequential difficulties for the sake of Christ, His Church, and His world. The lesson to be learned is that we are first and primarily Christians—and only then liberals or conservatives.

CHAPTER 16

A Catholic Approach to the Race Problem

There are many issues the layman can avoid in contemporary America if he tries hard enough. He may politely change the subject when religion is mentioned. Or he may cleverly label himself as an "independent" when politics comes up for discussion. But he cannot, try as he might, side-step having to take—directly or by implication—a stand on the issue of interracial justice.

The issue is always with us. The sights and sounds of marching troops in Little Rock or Montgomery are still in our ears. The harsh fate of Freedom Riders in Mississippi and Georgia cannot be erased from our memories. The smell of tear gas is in our nostrils. We can almost reach out and touch the cotton curtain of prejudice and race hatred that has been drawn around the South and some parts of the North.

In sophisticated, polite society we have managed to keep a veneer over the more outrageous forms of racial injustice. But we must face up to the fact that men who righteously regard themselves as good, practicing Christians do negate their very Christianity by acts of injustice and hatred. They speak out for democracy and then fight to keep Negroes from becoming their neighbor or their co-worker or the man in the voting booth next to them. Knowingly or not, they are direct descendants of the hypocrites so deservedly condemned by Christ Himself. To them I would apply the words of Isaias, quoted by Our Lord: "This people honors me with their lips, but their heart is far from me" (Mark 7:6).

Woe unto those who deny by their actions the words of Christ spoken to them through their Church and indeed through their own American bishops on the sinfulness of discrimination and prejudice. Racism and totalitarianism, said Pius XII, are twin evils of our day, and both are to be condemned. Condemned not just by words but by our very actions as well.

We have talked long enough. Now is the time for prudent, dedicated Christian action. We have our mandate from the Church; we have been told by our own bishops in their statement on discrimination in 1958 that "it is vital that we act now and act decisively. All must act quietly, courageously, and prayerfully before it is too late."

And to act effectively we must understand what the problem is all about and how a Christian should approach it.

We must look at the problem whole. We must see it as part of a network of social, economic, and moral problems that beset our society today. And to put our finger on the principles that should guide and direct our thinking, I suggest that we study carefully that great social document, Pius XI's *Quadragesimo Anno*.

In this valuable encyclical, Pius XI demonstrates the need for the reform of morals and the reform of institutions as the two foundation stones for the reconstruction of society. If we are to construct a decent society, we must work for both of these reforms. The application of these two lines of approach to race relations is as clear as their application to economic life, a fact which demonstrates their universality as effective tools in attempting to achieve solutions for every major social problem.

The race problem is itself made of two distinct, though related, elements: *prejudice* and *discrimination*.

Prejudice is primarily a personal, moral problem. True, it is tied in with a complex of psychological, cultural, and social attitudes and considerations, but it always boils down to the individual who is prejudiced.

Discrimination, on the other hand, is found in the very fabric of society. It is the practical outward expression of prejudice. It is the "institutional" part of the twofold approach of moral and institutional reform. Discrimination involves the laws and social customs which treat Negroes and other minority groups as if they were not quite human, not quite full-fledged Americans. It is, in other words, institutionalized prejudice. That is, it has become more or less permanently ingrained into our social habits and institutions.

Jim Crow, for example, is a case of discrimination. It is bigger than an individual's prejudice. It is an institutionalized part of Southern culture with legal sanctions attached to shore it up. Segregation in education is another instance, as are the poll tax and the many more subtle forms of discrimination which hold the Negroes' freedom and civil rights in a paralyzing embrace.

In addition, a vicious by-product of these institutions of discrimination is that they tend to perpetuate prejudice.

Take the case of segregation in the armed forces. In the past, before segregation in the service was abolished, the very fact that whites and Negroes were segregated tended to sustain the prejudice in the minds of whites that they were superior and that Negroes were naturally inferior.

Now that segregation has been eliminated, observers report that Negroes and whites get along reasonably well and that they usually accept each other as equals, many times forming fast friendships. This experience, which is the result of the good institution of integration, tends to eradicate, to lessen racial prejudice.

But when servicemen are discharged they are thrust back into a segregated society. Their service experience may have taught them how to get along in an interracial social situation and perhaps may have brought them to know and like Negroes. But they will have to be brave men indeed to stand up under the derision and pressures that will come to them if they attempt to fight the institutions of discrimination in their own home towns and try to mingle freely with Negroes or treat them as equals.

The majority of us are born compromisers and practicing realists. So most of us passively accept discrimination and go through the socially accepted motions of acting as if we were superior even if we don't feel that way. And our bad example, halfhearted as it may be, not only helps others to grow in prejudice, but it also helps perpetuate the very institutions of discrimination. This is a practical and concrete example of why Pius XI insisted on both moral reform and the reform of our social institutions, our social habits, as well. They belong together; they influence each other; each is necessary for a complete solution of any social problem.

Prejudice is a personal problem requiring moral reform. Discrimination is a problem of institutions, of social customs that require institutional reform. Because the race problem is made up of two parts, it requires a twofold solution, two kinds of approaches.

There is work for what Arnold Lunn in A *Saint in the Slave Trade* calls the divinitarian, the person mainly interested in the individual, in personal, moral reform. And also there is need of the social reformer who is primarily interested in the reconstruction of institutions.

In addition to charting the outlines of the race question, to help us understand it more incisively, Pius XI proposed for us two virtues that should be of particular significance to both the divinitarian and the social reformer in their work for the solution of the problem. And these two virtues are social justice and social charity.

Social justice aims at organized action to reconstruct the social order in a manner that recognizes the needs and aspirations of the human being. It demands that each individual take every appropriate action to achieve the common good. This means that as individuals and as groups we must work for the reform of unchristian institutions. Or where no institutions or social customs have yet been established we must set up good ones. This, I believe, especially applies in the case of brand-new housing developments and suburbs now springing up, where it should be easier to influence a community that does not have long-standing traditions and institutions of discrimination.

It is incumbent upon us not only to work for the reform of

existing institutions such as segregated schools and housing, but also to set up desirable institutions of our own, such as interracial centers and councils that create a social situation and social pressures conducive to charity and understanding.

Besides social justice, there is also social charity, which has been described as an unselfish and prodigal concern for the common good. This virtue aims at making us take an unselfish and helpful attitude toward our fellow members of society for the sake of their souls. It is the good will, tolerance, and patience that help to encourage and unify us in our work of social justice. It makes our personal love of God overflow into a social love of our fellow men, fanning to a white heat our desire to change or replace any social institution or custom that keeps them from loving God completely.

The Church has proclaimed the principles of interracial justice for years, but we as lay people have failed to translate these principles into the social customs and laws that will help make them a living reality. The clergy cannot normally act directly on society in the same way we can. Through the work of Catholic Interracial Councils, for example, the Church can preach the principles, she can carry on the great work of moral education, which is her special province. But in the normal course of events, unless we take these principles and make them a part of the laws of our society, the attitudes of our neighborhood, the customs of our social groups, these principles of Christ shall remain lifeless and ineffectual.

"Work at the building of a new world," said Cardinal Suhard; "it depends on you whether it will be Christian or not."

Will we work at this task of building a bright new Christian world? Will we be willing to speak out and be heard, even at personal expense? Will a great cry of anguish go up from us so that the world will know what we Catholics think of the scandal of racial injustice?

Some years ago in the New York *Times Magazine*, Hans J. Morgenthau had an article in which he expressed concern over the lack of moral indignation on the part of the American people over the TV scandals case. As a result, he received a letter from some students at Columbia University who asked that they not be identified as the authors of the letter.

Respecting their wishes to be kept anonymous, Mr. Morgenthau nonetheless answered them publicly in an article in the *New Republic*. He was speaking primarily to college students, but his words could be heeded just as profitably by all of us. He said:

"But imagine for a moment where man would be if his most intelligent, best educated, and most secure children had throughout history hidden their faces and spoken only in whispers. The great men whose lives and works you study are remembered exactly because they were not anonymous, because they showed their faces above the crowd and spoke in a loud voice all by themselves.

"What they spoke was more often than not the opposite of what the crowd believed and wanted to hear, and many of them lived in prison or in exile and died in disgrace or on the cross.

"Have you ever heard of two German students by the name of Huber, brother and sister, who openly defied Hitler in the University of Munich and were hanged? Do you not remember the Hungarian, East German, Polish and even Russian students who risked everything for their convictions and many of whom paid for them with their freedom and their lives?

"And you, risking nothing at all, refuse to speak above an anonymous whisper! Why are you so frightened by your own faces and your own voices?"

Why is it that the American layman is so often frightened by his own face and voice, refusing to speak above an anonymous whisper? As Christians in our innermost heart, we must sooner or later ask ourself: What would Christ have me do? How would Christ have acted if He were in my place in the world today? Would He keep silent? Would He be willing to make personal sacrifices, if necessary, to fight for the cause of justice?

No one need tell us the answers to these questions. We all know the answers.

There was a day when martyrdom meant being thrown to

the lions or losing your head for your Faith. Things have changed today and we relegate lions to the zoo, but martyrdom is still available to those brave enough to risk it and Christian witnesses are still as necessary as they were nineteen centuries ago.

Our martyrdom might be something as simple and as unpleasant as being shunned by family and friends. Or it may even mean incurring the wrath of an employer. But we must start somewhere! We must take action. It is not enough to organize study clubs in which the bishops' statement on discrimination is read and dissected and analyzed and agreed with. We must *act* in our everyday lives as if we believed the teachings of Christ.

There is work for the voter and organizer and legislator who will fight to change and reform these social institutions in which hatred has become incarnate. And there is work for those who will simply be present where they are needed, who will show forth to the Negro the love of Christ. Each of us has an indispensable task, a job which no one else can perform for us; and if we will not do it, if we fail our God and our Church it will not be done.

I said at the beginning of this chapter that the challenge of interracial justice is one issue the layman cannot avoid today in American society. For even if he manages to dodge open discussion of it, it is so omnipresent that either by action or by failure to speak up when he should he will be forced to take a stand. And our bishops have made it crystal-clear in their 1958 statement that there is only one stand the Christian may take on the race question. Twist and turn as we might, there is only one position the layman may hold in the face of discrimination and injustice.

And for the responsible layman it is not enough merely to be for interracial justice in principle or with words only. Our bishops showed us the course to follow when they said: ". . . we hope and earnestly pray that responsible and sober-minded Americans of all religious faiths, in all areas of our land, will seize the mantle of leadership from the agitator and the racist.

It is vital that we act now and act decisively. All must act quietly, courageously and prayerfully before it is too late."

The times cry out for the voices of all good men to be heard. For Christian voices to be heard on the side of Christ. Silence can be golden. It can also be just plain yellow.

CHAPTER 17

Censorship and Catholics

Asked to speak on the subject of "Freedom and Christian Responsibility," a Catholic editor began by telling of the similarity between his assignment and the two GI's who were seeing the Atlantic Ocean for the first time.

"What a lot of water!" said Joe.

"You ain't seen nothing yet," answered Willie. "That's just the surface!"

The Catholic concerned about censorship also "ain't seen nothing yet" if he believes that censorship is a relatively simple problem with easy answers. Indeed, before a Catholic (particularly in the United States) is allowed even to enter into a public discussion of censorship, I believe he should first be subjected to a rigorous indoctrination into the history and meaning of civil liberties. For censorship can only be understood in America within the context of our democratic concern for freedom.

These liberties, which we call civil, are those with which the first ten and the fourteenth amendments to the Constitution are concerned. Our freedom of speech, religion, press, right of petition, and other rights are covered in the first ten amendments. Among other things, the Fourteenth Amendment guarantees us "due process of law" and "equal protection of the laws." Included in the idea of civil liberties are "civil rights," which are civil liberties especially as they refer to Negroes and other minority groups.

Catholics have a special stake in the cause of civil liberties. "Everything in our religion should impel us to be concerned about this matter," Dean Joseph O'Meara, Jr., of the University of Notre Dame Law School, told me once in an interview on the subject. And he quoted a few excerpts from a 1960 pastoral letter of the bishops of the Dominican Republic:

". . . the basis and foundation of all positive law is the inviolable dignity of the human person. . . . His Holiness Pope Pius XII . . . declared on a certain occasion with regard to liberty that it was the proper climate for the realization of the natural rights of man. . . . We do not want, most beloved brethren, to burden you unduly and we comment only briefly on the other natural rights which accompany those to which we have alluded, namely, the rights of all men to freedom of conscience, the press, and assembly.

"To recognize these natural rights, to teach them and to put them into effect to their full material and spiritual perfection, is the sublime mission of civil authority and of ecclesiastical authority, each working in its proper sphere and with the proper means.

"The contrary to this constitutes a grave offense against God, against the dignity of man—made in the image and likeness of his Creator—and brings about many and irreparable evils in society."

"It seems to me," Dean O'Meara commented, "that this is a kind of textbook for Catholics in civil liberties. The concern of our religion for the spiritual, social, political and economic rights of the individual should make every Catholic a defender of every man's civil liberties. If Catholics are not concerned about civil liberties, I am afraid it is because they do not really understand the meaning of their religion; at least they do not comprehend fully its spirit."

Because "freedom is indivisible" (to use Dean O'Meara's words) Catholics must be equally concerned with civil liberties as well as with censorship. This was brought out by the dean when I asked him if, because the First Amendment protects the advocacy of ideas, men should be free to advocate the ideas, for example, that Jews should be put in concentration camps, that Negroes be lynched or that Catholics be excluded from public office?

"What is the alternative?" he replied. "We do not like the

ideas you mentioned, but the same freedom that gives men the right to advocate those ideas protects us in our right to advocate our ideas. As I said earlier, freedom is indivisible. And what gives me reason for concern occasionally is the tendency I detect on the part of some Catholics not to be willing to give to others the rights they want for themselves. It is true to say that error has no rights, but *people* do."

There is reason for concern also in terms of the image of the Church, the view that we project to others of what the Church is like. Catholics are always there to stand up and be counted when it comes to establishing an anti-pornography group. Some Catholic groups take direct and indirect action against book and magazine sellers. And it is not too exaggerated to say that some Catholic laymen give the impression to non-Catholics that the main task of the Church is to enforce her interpretation of the Sixth and Ninth Commandments, particularly as they apply to books, magazines, and movies.

Let it be understood that there is nothing un-American or unchristian in principle in being for censorship or control of pornography. The problem—in terms of the image of the Church—arises when Catholics seem to show not the slightest interest in freedom and liberty but seem to demonstrate an almost morbid preoccupation with obscenity. Balance could so easily be restored to the public portrait of the Church in the eyes of outsiders who are potential members if only we would more often declare ourselves by word and action on the side of the civil liberties, which protect and nourish us and our religion.

Censorship, therefore, is but the tip of the iceberg. Beneath it lies the complex, complicated, and still completely uncharted vastness of civil liberties. Even censorship as it relates to pornography alone is filled with complexity and also with a regularly recurrent note of public controversy. Accordingly, it can be most instructive for the modern Catholic layman to learn more about what is going to continue to be a thorn in the side of both interreligious understanding and the democratic process, which is constantly engaged in the battle to reconcile private rights and public interest.

To begin at the beginning, let us attempt to define what we mean by censorship. In his excellent *Catholic Viewpoint on Censorship*, Father Harold C. Gardiner, S.J., describes the way in which he uses it in his book: "The power to disagree and then enforce that disagreement through some channel of authority—in short, the exercise of control—is, then, the sense in which the word 'censorship' will be employed in all that follows. It would truly make for clarity of argument if all —the National Legion of Decency, the National Office for Decent Literature, the American Civil Liberties Union, the American Book Publishers Council and all agencies concerned in the discussion—would resolve to discard the word 'censorship' and adopt the word 'control.' 'Censorship,' strictly so called, can be exercised in our American constitutional framework only through legal channels; but control is exercised, and must be exercised, through channels that are 'extra-legal,' though never anti-legal. In other words, the state, through judges and courts, can alone bring censorship to bear on the problem of 'indecent' literature and films; but society can and does bring 'control' to bear long before the judges and the courts can or ought to be called into the dispute."

A primary concern in the problem of censorship is the idea of *prior* censorship, that is, the *prevention* of something being seen or published or distributed. It is not censorship, for example, when a group such as the Legion of Decency classifies, according to certain moral criteria, movies that are already being distributed.

The real problem, of course, is not how to define censorship. Or how to prevent it. Any realistic observer is forced to conclude that we have always had censorship and various controls; we have it now and we shall continue to have it in the future. Despite public statements to the contrary, I really cannot believe that most Americans will ever reach the stage where they genuinely won't want or allow *any* kind of censorship on *any* level. The real issue is how to supervise the inevitable censorship we shall always have so that it will not violate men's civil liberties and all the political realities that are dependent on these liberties.

The root problem is one of balance. As citizens, we love our freedom and our hard-won civil liberties. We insist on preserving and extending them, for we know how closely linked one liberty is with all the rest. As Catholics we have an added incentive: We want all men to be as free as possible to seek the God whose absence makes their heart grow restless; we desire the opportunity for all men to make their freedom meaningful by freely and voluntarily conforming to the law of God. The free gift of a soul, freely given, has, I believe, more worth than all the legislated morality the mind of man can conceive.

But as parents and as citizens we know that freedom has to have limits. We do not want men free to corrupt our children with filth and obscenity. We want some reasonable restraints against those who would destroy us, our children, our way of life. How can we exercise control to protect ourselves on the one hand without at the same time destroying, on the other, the very liberties that make life worth-while?

As Americans we would die to preserve the rights covered in the First Amendment—freedom of religion, speech, press, assembly, and to petition the government for redress. As Dean O'Meara commented about these rights:

"The reason, of course, why these are so important is that these are the presuppositions of a democracy. Our democracy depends on these rights if it is going to exist at all, so we must keep a close guard over these foundation stones of our entire democratic way of life. It is one of the presuppositions of democracy that men will speak their minds; it is one of the conditions of democracy that all sides of public questions will be heard. Thus, it is one of the obligations of citizenship to speak out for what one believes. It is the democratic thesis that in this way over the years error is best combated."

Because freedom, liberty, and censorship have far-reaching moral implications, it is also important to know what guidance the Church can give us on this problem. Father Gardiner sums it up admirably:

". . . When one is asked, 'What does *the Church* think of censorship?' one can only respond, 'Let's look at the law and its spirit.' Obviously, in the application of that law to a particular country and to a particular age, there will be variations —never in essentials, but in accidentals. But *the Church*, speaking in its official capacity, has no opinion on the operations of civil censorship. Not on the *operations*; but the Church may very well have strong opinions on a philosophy that underlies either censorship or the lack of it. The whole tradition and spirit of the Church would deny that legitimate governments have no *right* to censor for the common good; that tradition and spirit would indeed assert the *duty* of such governments to censor for that same good. On the other hand, the Church would deny the *right* of any government to censor any truth—intellectual or moral—as a matter of policy, or to broadcast any error in the same manner."

Thus, we can see that censorship has two important dimensions—the spiritual and the temporal or civil. The Church establishes the spiritual meaning of freedom and the moral right and duty of the state to exercise some form of censorship and control for the sake of all. Note that the Church *does not* prescribe any particular form of censorship in the civil order. She is concerned primarily with establishing the right; she is not interfering in the administration of the temporal affairs of men; rather, she is making their work easier by helping to set up the moral limits and goals in relation to this matter. It is left up to the competence of the temporal order to devise its own best means of carrying out its right and duty to censor for the common good.

And in the practical application of principle and practice in the temporal order, we come face to face again with the problem of achieving a balance. "The issue that is central in the whole problem is the issue of social freedom," Jesuit theologian John Courtney Murray told the Thomas More Association of Chicago in 1956. "More exactly," he continued, "it is the issue of striking a right balance between freedom and restraint in society. This is the most difficult problem of social science, to such an extent that all other difficulties are reducible to this one."

In the same address, Father Murray, in a few brief paragraphs, said some things about the indivisibility of freedom that should be made required reading for every American citizen. He observed:

" . . . The fact is that the imposition of constraints, the limitation of freedom, has consequences. They are numerous, but two require special notice.

"First, if you impose a constraint on freedom in one domain, in order to increase freedom in another, you may take the risk of damaging freedom in a third domain, with consequences more dangerous to the community. Social freedom is a complex, whose constituent elements are closely interlocked. You may, for instance, wish to 'clean up' political campaigns by limiting the freedom of the contestants to attack each other's personal integrity; but the means you take to this end may damage the freedom of the electoral process itself. Every constraint has multiple effects; it may impose restraints on a freedom which you would wish to see untouched.

"There is, secondly, a consequent consideration. Because social freedoms interlock so tightly, it is not possible to know antecedently what the multiple effects of a regulation will be. At best, the effect you want can only be foreseen with probability, not certainty. And unforeseen effects may follow, with the result that a regulation, in itself sensible, may in the end do more harm than good.

"For this reason, the social reformer whose only strength is a sense of logic may well be a menace. For instance, if drunkenness and alcoholism are social vices whose effect is to diminish and impair the free will of men (as indeed they are), the logical thing is to ban alcohol. Here in America we learned by experience the disastrous effects of that type of mad logic."

The American Catholic layman often goes through many changes in his attitudes toward freedom and censorship, be-

ginning with the "logic" described by Father Murray. When
he is young and unsophisticated, the issue seems quite clear
and he looks at it in black and white moral terms: "Dirty"
books, movies, and magazines are immoral in intent and effect; therefore, they should be removed from circulation. The
next step is when the layman discovers, through reading or experience, the exigencies and demands of the democratic process in a pluralistic society; he enters into the world of civil
liberties. As he grows older and his children begin to be faced
with the problem of off-color or obscene books, magazines, or
movies, the problem is presented again on a higher and more
subtle level. He wishes neither to abandon his children nor his
civil liberties. He is then faced with the cold reality of balanc-
ing freedom and constraint. He does not want to sacrifice his
political freedoms, but does this mean that to save them he
must sacrifice his children to the corrupters, the smut peddlers,
the pornographers? What is the way out? Where is he to turn
for guidance?

Well, one place is the little known 1957 statement of the
American bishops on censorship, which blends both moral and
political common sense:

"Ideally," the bishops say, "we could wish that no man-
made legal restraints were ever necessary. Thus, restraint on
any human freedom would be imposed rather by one's own
reason than by external authority. In any case, restraint's best
justification is that it is imposed for the sake of a greater freedom. Since, however, individuals do act in an irresponsible
way and do threaten social and moral harm, society must face
its responsibility and exercise its authority. The exigencies of
social living demand it."

They comment further:

"Although civil authority has the right and duty to exercise
such control over the various media of communication as is
necessary to safeguard public morals, yet civil law, especially
in those areas which are constitutionally protected, will define
as narrowly as possible the limitations placed on freedom. The
one purpose which will guide legislators in establishing neces-

sary restraints to freedom is the securing of the general welfare through the prevention of grave and harmful abuse. Our juridical system has been dedicated from the beginning to the principle of minimal restraint. Those who may become impatient with the reluctance of the state through its laws to curb and curtail human freedom should bear in mind that this is a principle which serves to safeguard all our vital freedoms—to curb less rather than more; to hold for liberty rather than for restraint.

"In practice, the exercise of any such curbs by the state calls for the highest discretion and prudence. This is particularly true in the area of the press. For here an unbridled power to curb and repress can make a tyrant of government, and can wrest from the people one by one their most cherished liberties.

"Prudence will always demand, as is true under our governmental system, that the courts be in a position to protect the people against arbitrary repressive action. While they uphold the authority of government to suppress that which not only has no social value but is actually harmful, as is the case with the obscene, the courts will be the traditional bulwark of the people's liberties."

Every responsible authoritative source urges and counsels us not to use rash or illegal means to combat the very real dangers that censorship can defend us from. They argue that the indivisibility and unity of liberty is such that a greater and more lasting harm may result to the common good from ill-considered action than from the existence of censorable materials. If we take their advice, we are left then with two possible major courses of action—a positive and a negative one.

On the negative side, we may work as individuals and through groups for the enforcement of existing anti-obscenity laws. This is one of the major functions of the quiet, but often effective, Citizens for Decent Literature, founded in Cincinnati in 1956 and active nationally since 1960. A great deal of CDL's effectiveness springs from the June 24, 1957, *Roth* decision of the United States Supreme Court, which gave this test as to whether material is legally obscene: "Whether to the average person, applying contemporary community standards, the dominant theme of the material taken as a whole appeals to prurient interest." (Prurient is "a shameful or morbid interest in nudity, sex, or excretion.")

In the *Roth* decision the Court also reached another notable conclusion, namely, that obscenity does not come under the constitutional guarantees of freedom of speech and the press. It explained:

"All ideas having even the slightest redeeming social importance—unorthodox ideas, controversial ideas, even ideas hateful to the prevailing climate of opinion—have the full protection of the guaranties, unless excludable because they encroach upon the limited area of more important interests. But implicit in the history of the first amendment is the rejection of obscenity as utterly without redeeming social importance."

CDL founder, Charles H. Keating, Jr., of Cincinnati, explains: "When the public clearly shows that it considers filthy and revolting publications unfit for our society, the courts are greatly aided." Thus, a good deal of the work of the Citizens for Decent Literature has been educational, explaining the dangers of pornography and giving public support to the police and legal agencies in their investigations, arrests, and prosecution of obscenity cases. The CDL has also, for example, provided the court with the volunteer testimony of expert witnesses (e.g., psychiatrists and psychologists). It is attempting to make known to the courts at least on the local level what "contemporary community standards" are.

There is every reason to believe that, generally, CDL's methods have been effective, restrained, and admirable. But they are certainly no panacea. This fact was demonstrated by a unique seminar toward the end of 1961 sponsored by *Catholic World* on "Freedom of Speech and Obscenity Censorship." A discussion there of the "effects" controversy indicated that many psychiatrists deny that a casual relationship may be demonstrated between reading pornography and sex crimes. As the editor of *Catholic World* observed in summarizing the controversy: "Our courts proceed on the assumption that reading obscenity does cause these crimes but the conscientious jurist is reluctant to convict a news vendor on the strength of a dubious presumption that is under attack from psychiatrists."

The same seminar also brought out other difficulties with the legal approach. For one, there is good reason to believe that "community standards" as used by the Court refers to the national rather than the local community. And the question was also raised by one priest-participant as to whether these standards themselves could be too low because of the very dark picture painted of American morals by various sociological studies.

This means, then, that we must put continued and simultaneous emphasis on *positive* courses of action.

In any study of the problem of censorship and indecency it becomes immediately apparent that most of the sexy magazines, dirty paperbacks, or suggestive movies are not legally obscene. For the amount of hard core pornography that can be handled by existing laws is relatively small when compared to the thousands and thousands of newsstands and drugstores throughout the nation which flaunt the kind of erotic and sexually stimulating literature common sense and experience tells us do not lend themselves to the building of character or a healthy attitude toward sex. The bishops advert to this in their 1957 statement when they observe:

"Within the bounds essential to the preservation of a free press, human action and human expression may fall short of what is legally punishable and may still defy the moral standards of a notable number in the community. Between the legally punishable and the morally good there exists a wide gap. If we are content to accept as morally inoffensive all that is legally unpunishable, we have lowered greatly our moral standards. It must be recognized that civil legislation by itself does not constitute an adequate standard of morality."

Closing the gap the bishops refer to is the primary work of the positive approach. In our own family circle, through our educational institutions, through libraries, through the communications media—by every means at our disposal—we must work to promote good taste and a general sense of decency in literature and all the arts among the public at large. By building up a desire and appreciation for what is good—a goal which is desirable in itself—we may hope to eliminate some of the corrupting power of the indecent by educating the community to realize that its inartistic base and lack of taste are repugnant aesthetically as well as morally. Although the scope of the problem is wide and broad, we can take hope from the fact that the means to meet it are equally extensive, limited only by our enthusiasm, dedication, and imagination.

It may prove discouraging for some if we point out that the censorship problem is not a problem we shall ever solve once for all, simply because it is part of the fundamental problem of social freedom and civil liberties. No one generation can ever solve these problems, for they are too bound to current problems and events to permit a permanent solution. In a way, each generation has to solve the problem for itself in terms of its own special requirements. The question of freedom and restraint will be as vital during the 2060s as it is proving to be during the 1960s.

Thus far, we have barely begun to scratch the surface that Willie talked about at the beginning of this chapter. We have hardly begun to plumb the depths of censorship and pornography, much less the broader aspects of censorship and the parent problems of civil liberties and restraint and freedom. But the information we have considered should at least have led us to the development of some attitudes. For one, we must cultivate an attitude of the greatest respect for civil liberties, never treating them lightly, no matter how desirable or "moral" our immediate goal. And wherever possible we should do whatever is in our power to promote the positive, to advance the cause of the appreciation of the arts, both because they are good in themselves and because of the secondary effects their appreciation engenders.

Father Murray said it well in his address to the Thomas More Association:

"It is a good thing to keep our problems in perspective. Our chief problem, of course, is not literary censorship, but literary creation. This is true in the Church. She has no trouble in finding censors; but she prays continually that God may give her men of learning who can write the works that need to be written. The American Catholic community particularly needs to attend seriously to this problem of literary creation. Leo XIII is indeed remembered for his revision of the Index of Forbidden Books. But he was not the first Pope to point to the dangers of reading bad books. It is his great glory that he was the first Pope to say, in substance and effect, in a multitude of discourses, that today there is great danger in not reading good books. This is why I think it is a fine thing for the Thomas More Association to sponsor a lecture on censorship —once every seventeen years!"

CHAPTER 18

True Anti-Communism

Ever since the 1930s and the days of the Dies' Committee and succeeding congressional investigations of un-American affairs, Americans have been swept along periodically by waves of anti- and anti-anti-communism. On the one hand, the cleverness of the communist apparatus in the United States in camouflaging its activities and in spreading confusion has left many Americans confused about the communist issue. And, unfortunately, the occasional self-seeking of a relatively few publicity-conscious members of congressional committees has also sometimes thrown up a smoke screen of doubt about communism and communists in the United States.

The American Catholic layman, however, should have no doubt about where the Church stands on the communist issue. As far back as 1846, in *Qui Pluribus*, Pius IX solemnly condemned "that infamous doctrine of communism, which is absolutely contrary to the natural law itself, and, if once adopted, would utterly destroy the rights, property, and possessions of all men, and even society itself." In 1891, in his famous *Rerum Novarum*, Leo XIII went into great detail to refute the errors of Marxian socialism.

Note that this was before the modern international conspiracy led by the Communist Party in Soviet Russia. To deal with this modern situation, Pius XI, after touching briefly on the subject in his encyclical *Quadragesimo Anno* in 1931, followed this a few years later, in 1937, with a detailed exposition of communism and a positive program for our guidance in fighting it, namely, his encyclical *Divini Redemptoris*, (*On Atheistic Communism*).

Pope Pius XII directly and indirectly approached the problem of communism many times during his reign. Even his very first encyclical, *Summi Pontificatus*, in 1939 was concerned with the twin evils of racism and totalitarianism. And, of course, in 1949 Pius XII issued the decree which *ipso facto* excommunicated as apostates Catholics "who profess, defend, and spread the materialistic and anti-Christian doctrine of the Communists." And, most recently, Pope John XXIII issued the longest social encyclical ever published dealing with the social doctrine of the Church, which is opposed to communist social principles.

Since the very beginning of communism and, later, the organized communist conspiracy in the Soviet Union and also internationally, the Church has recognized the evil for what it is and has used every means at her disposal to battle the materialistic and essentially anti-Christian forces of communism. Compared to the Church's long-term campaign against communist machinations, most of us today are a Rip Van Winkle-ish lot of Johnny-come-latelys.

What does this mean for the Catholic layman in America today? What can he do to fight communism? Where should he turn for help and guidance in seeking direction for his social thought and action?

Some of these questions might be answered best by asking another question: What if there were no communists? What if communism did not exist?

If such were the case, what kind of society should the Christian be working for? What kind of program would he be advancing? His concern for society and the future of his country and the world would not be built upon fear of communism; he could not predicate his goals on the existence of a communist menace, nationally or internationally.

Without doubt the fact that an international communist conspiracy does exist does indeed change the picture of life in America and the world in the 1960s. But Christianity stands condemned by its own sterility if its only goals are defensive and built on a negative anti-communist program. Fortunately, the Church does have a program aimed at the construction of a society impregnated and guided by the virtues of justice and love. And the program, the social way of life the Church offers is to be found primarily in Catholic social doctrine especially as formulated over the last century by the popes. In our times the four most immediately pertinent and valuable treatments by the pontiffs—though these are by no means the only sources of papal thought on communism—are: Leo XIII's *Rerum Novarum*, Pius XI's *Quadragesimo Anno* and *Divini Redemptoris*, and Pope John's *Mater et Magistra*.

From these documents we get the general picture of the Church's approach to the fight against communism: In the construction of a Christian society we follow two lines of action: moral and social reform, the reform of individuals and the reform of society, the building up of private and public morals; and the positive creation of a society which does not violate the basic social principles of Christianity and, indeed, which permits and promotes the cultivation of the supernatural.

There is also a negative element introduced, concerned principally with educating people to the dangers and evils of communism, its infiltration into important areas of public life and the dangers it presents. This combined negative-positive method is summed up well by Pius XI in the advice he gives (in *Divini Redemptoris*) to the Catholic press on how to fight communism. He says: "Its foremost duty is to foster in various attractive ways an even better understanding of social doctrine. It should, too, supply accurate and complete information on the activity of the enemy and the means of resistance which have been found most effective in various quarters. It should offer useful suggestions and warn against the insidious deceits with which Communists endeavor, all too successfully, to attract even men of good faith."

By turning to the papal social documents, then, we learn that the popes are preoccupied with the idea of building a Christian society through the combined changing of individuals and of society; both the individual and the social (or institutional) apostolates are essential links in the chain. Pope

John makes it quite clear in *Mater et Magistra* that this positive emphasis on building a decent society is an essential and dynamic answer to the communist challenge, in addition to its own intrinsic merit.

In practice, though, the major problem facing the American Catholic layman who is attempting to make up his mind on how best to fight communism is usually polarized in this way: Should I devote most of my time to the negative or the positive way of fighting communism?

It seems to be demonstrable that a considerable number of today's Catholics prefer the negative approach of informing people of the dangers of communism and educating them on its theory and practice. Various explanations have been given of why this is so. One of the most widely accepted of these explanations is that Catholics still tend to be regarded as "immigrant" groups and thus in reaction to this they are consciously or unconsciously trying to prove how American they are by joining and playing an active role in patriotic and anti-communist organizations.

Be that as it may, there is nothing wrong with devoting time and energy to the negative approach; it is an essential part of every anti-communist program. The danger lies in lack of balance. This can be illustrated in part by a letter I received once from a reader who commented on an editorial I had published in a Catholic magazine on the pressing need for a positive approach to anti-communism and the promotion of love and justice and making these a part of society today for love of God. Her comments might be perused at length because they are both sincere and typical.

She wrote: "It seems that you are among those who hold the fallacy that the fight against communism can be carried on successfully in a 'positive' way by the application of the Popes' social encyclicals. At this moment in history, I think something 'negative' is necessary to fight communism, so that we can be *free* to work 'for the establishment of justice and love in the world' now and in the many years it will take to accomplish this goal.

"Furthermore, if it be true (as many authorities insist) that communism makes its best progress not among the poor and underprivileged but among a nation's intellectuals, are we then going to eliminate communism simply by raising the standard of living among the poor of the world? It is not that simple. The Communists do not need a people with a low standard of living to take control of a country! They will succeed in ours if we do nothing.

" . . . I think a type of precaution against Communist infiltration and treachery that Pius XI would approve would be a study group in which its members would learn to recognize Communist tactics and to prevent their country being taken over and unable very shortly to do anything to raise *anyone*'s standard of living—even their own!"

This letter raises many questions that are frequently on the minds of Catholics today in their concern about communism.

First, it is quite clear that the negative approach is respectable and necessary. The study of communist theory, strategy, and tactics, dialectical materialism, the class struggle, the communist program, the international conspiracy, and all the rest are worth-while projects. The question that arises, though, is again one of balance. How effective can we be against communism by the use of the negative approach? Is the real threat to us from communism primarily internal or external?

The debate over this will probably never be settled. We can be certain that the communists will do all within their power, now and in the future, to subvert our nation by every fair and foul means. There is need for constant vigilance. Yet, there seems to be a preponderance of evidence today that the greatest threat to us posed by the Reds is external rather than internal. Father John F. Cronin, S.S., assistant director of the Social Action Department of the National Catholic Welfare Conference and a recognized authority in both Catholic and secular circles on communism, wrote in *America*:

" . . . most students of communism report that the area of danger today is external, not domestic. The Communist problem is real and critical in Latin America, Asia and Africa. It is so serious, in fact, that many competent observers feel that the next ten years may be decisive. There is a distinct possibility that, within a decade, the entire Southern hemisphere may be substantially within the Communist camp. If this analysis is correct, exclusive concentration upon domestic communism would be helping, not hurting, whatever plans Moscow and Peiping have.

"Second, there is the fact that the Communist Party in the United States has been seriously weakened in the last ten years. Its present claimed membership is 10,000. There are reasons to believe that this figure is exaggerated. The *Daily Worker* is no longer published. Only a very few Communist-front groups are active. Communist influence in the labor movement is negligible. Except for attempted espionage operations, which are controlled by foreign Communist governments, there is no evidence of current Communist penetration into government or the armed forces."

This is not to say that there is no home-grown communist danger confronting us today. But it does substantiate the opinion that the negative approach to communism today has less to concentrate on within our frontiers than in the past and that our positive efforts are especially needed at home and abroad. Further, there is the April 17, 1961, statement of FBI director J. Edgar Hoover on internal security, which noted that "individual Communists are difficult to recognize" and asked: "Do not circulate rumors about subversive activities or draw conclusions from information coming to your attention. The data you possess may be incomplete or only partially accurate, and by drawing conclusions or circulating rumors you can cause grave injustices to innocent persons. Hysteria, witch hunts, and vigilante activities weaken our security. It is just as important to protect the innocent as it is to identify our enemies." He requested also: "Refrain from making private investigations. Report the information you have to the FBI and leave the checking of the data to trained investigators. Indiscriminate inquiries might well jeopardize investigation already under way."

We must recognize that the negative approach is, in many ways, self-limiting. That is, much of it is a matter of police work in the hands of federal and other investigative agencies. Mr. Hoover lists some cogent reasons above as to why we must place certain phases of the negative approach in the hands of the proper authorities.

In an address to an anti-communist meeting in Chicago in 1961, another FBI man of great experience with the communists had similar advice to give. William Sullivan, chief inspector of the FBI in charge of investigating communist subversion, intelligence, and espionage, speaking on "The Internal Threat of Communism," cautioned against "vigilante action" by unqualified individuals. "The job of curtailing and containing communism is one for the legally constituted authorities," he said.

"Essentially what is needed," he added, "is a calm, dispassionate, informed approach to the problem. We must not merely react defensively to every shift in Communist tactics. We must place greater positive emphasis on eliminating the political, social and economic ills—political instability, economic unrest, religious and racial discrimination, educational deficiencies, corruption in public life, youthful criminality— which weaken the social fabric and make a community more susceptible to the specious appeals of communism."

Mr. Sullivan is probably as aware as any man in America of the actual dangers of the communist menace. In no way does he undervalue the threat. But like the papal social documents, he also recognizes the fact that we must "place greater positive emphasis" on building a just and decent society. Yet, our letter writer above, typical of many who share her views, questions the value of this. Since communism makes inroads among intellectuals, we cannot eliminate it "simply by raising the low standard of living among the poor of the world."

Well, as she says, "It is not that simple." I have never heard any one who emphasizes the positive approach say that the total answer to communism is raising low living standards. But we have only to turn to Latin America, where the world's eyes are currently frequently focused, to see the relationship between socio-economic conditions and the advance of communism—from Mexico City to Cape Horn. In the last decade one bishop after another South of the Border has deplored social injustices and the impetus they have given to the communist cause.

Typical of the reaction of many Latin American bishops is the statement by Bishop Manuel Larrain of Talca, Chile, reported in *Ave Maria:* "Shocking social inequality, the existence of immense proletarian and sub-proletarian masses living in inhuman conditions, the monopoly of land ownership . . . and the general lack of social awareness on the part of well-to-do Catholics. . . . With us, or without us, social reform is going to take place; in the latter event, it will take place against us."

Acting to implement their frequently stated views, at the end of 1961 the bishops of Chile announced plans to divide and sell all farms and estates belonging to Catholic dioceses in Chile to rural families. The bishops noted at the time they were eager to cooperate with the Chilean Government "not only by teaching the fundamental doctrine but also by giving concrete example," despite the financial sacrifices involved in their self-imposed plan.

The very existence of social injustices and instability, the lack of an economically secure citizenry who participate freely and actively in the affairs of their government is in itself a ready-made situation for the communist agitator. As Boston's Richard Cardinal Cushing told the Bolivian National Eucharistic Congress in 1961: By neglecting to establish a social order founded on justice and charity, "we shall prepare the way for the advance of atheistic communism."

So, let's have our negative approach, our study groups, and vigilance against communist infiltration, within the reasonable limits suggested above by Mr. Hoover. But let us not lose our sense of proportion. Let's not become so preoccupied with the negative that we forget or neglect the support of positive measures so especially demanded by the needs of our times.

In *The Third Revolution*, psychiatrist Karl Stern gives strong psychiatric support for the Popes' balanced positive and negative approach with a great deal of emphasis on the positive factors that are needed to defeat communism. Dr. Stern writes:

"Today, while we are facing the evil of communism, vigilance is more necessary than at any other time. Everybody agrees about that. But vigilance has a tendency to open, in a subtle and imperceptible way, frontiers in the human soul which had better be forever closed. Vigilance in the face of evil may give rise to preoccupation with evil. And, as the Fathers of the Church taught, if we are unduly preoccupied with evil, we become evil. There is danger in giving more thought to the things we are *against* than the things we are *for*. It is easier to have distrust than to have faith. The story of the early Church shows clearly that it is the positive in Faith which conquers the world.

". . . Today, when Communists and secret Communist machinations present an objective danger, we face a great pitfall. It is not a question of paranoia in the clinical sense. It is an imponderable something which happens to a community of Faith. We have our nose to the ground to ferret out the scent of the adversary; we have our ears to the ground to hear the distant rumbling; before we know it, something decisive has happened to us. We are no longer upright. Our gaze is no longer fixed on God and man in charity."

The balanced elements of Catholic social doctrine, however, avoid this preoccupation and its resultant dangers. And both Pius XI and Pope John have pleaded with us to make the social teachings of the Church understood and loved throughout every strata of the Church. Why is this positive approach so important at this time? In an address some years ago, Auxiliary Bishop John F. Hackett of Hartford, Connecticut, explained it when he said:

"We cannot be merely against Communists. We must be for the necessities of decent living—for a living family wage, for decent housing for all people, for interracial justice, for effective trade unions to protect man's rights, for labor-management cooperation and partnership, for the effective protection of the basic rights of all citizens. This is the type of anti-communism called for by the Holy Father in his encyclical called *Atheistic Communism*. This is the type of anti-communism which will be the only sound bulwark of liberty in today's world."

We must be concerned with this positive approach, the bishop added, "because we believe in God, because we believe all men are God's children, because we believe all men have the natural right to the necessities of decent living while on earth, we must protest—and protest far more eloquently than the Communists—these conditions which make impossible for millions the opportunity for a human standard of living."

Faced with the reality and challenge of communism today, as well as the possible variety of means by which he may work to combat it, the American Catholic layman must get his anti-communism from the Church if he is to be effective and thoroughly Christian in his response to the challenge. He must avoid one-sided approaches on both the right and the left and make his own the revolutionary and radical Christian social principles of the Church, revolutionary and radical in the sense that they get to the heart, the root, of the problem of communism, recognizing that atheistic communism is both an effect and a cause and that it is part of the larger anti-Christian problem of materialism and secularism that have infected the modern world.

The heresy of communism is the latest and probably the most virile and deadly of the heresies the Church has faced in her 2000 years of existence. To confront it head-on we must keep before us the words of Pius XI in 1931 that "unless utmost efforts are made without delay to put [Christian social principles] into effect, let no one persuade himself that public order, peace and tranquility of human society can be effectively defended against agitators of revolution." And his accusation in 1937: "There would be today neither socialism nor communism if the rulers of the nations had not scorned the teachings and the maternal warnings of the Church."

If we refuse to accept and act upon such clear-cut instructions and warnings I think we might well resign ourselves to the inevitability of the horrors of a communist victory over the free world.

CHAPTER 19

Peace and Internationalism

Peace, sweet peace. What would any sane man not do in these days of impending thermonuclear destruction to bring order and tranquility into our tormented, Cold War kind of world, a world which hangs midway between peace and war with a mushroom cloud as a ghoulish backdrop? Yet, most American Catholic laymen are hamstrung in their efforts for the peace they desire so urgently simply because they are ignorant of the existence of a considerable body of papal thought on how to secure the peace. Many of them were so busy fighting the war in the early 1940s and then returning to normal life afterward, they remain unaware that from the beginning of his pontificate in 1939 till his death almost two decades later Pius XII developed in detail the essentials for a workable peace plan. And he was following in the tradition of his predecessors who had since the turn of the century been actively concerned with international relations.

Because of this widespread ignorance that there is available a rather highly developed system of papal thought on peace, the efforts of Catholics to bring the peace of Christ to a world enmeshed in an atmosphere of non-peace are being dissipated and often given to causes which can only encourage tensions. As Catholics, we can hardly talk sensibly about peace without consulting Pius XII.

When we turn to this great Pontiff we note that he is called equally the Pope of Peace and the Pope of International Life. The reason is that the achievement of peace requires commitment to the principles of internationalism as defined and explained by Pius XII. In address and message after address and message, he made it clear that we must rid ourselves of

introverted ultranationalistic views, which turn us in upon
ourselves; instead, we must begin to develop an understanding
and concern of our relationship to other nations and to all
mankind. Typical of dozens upon dozens of other statements
that can easily be mustered is this excerpt from his 1948
Christmas Message:

"The Catholic doctrine on the state and civil society has
always been based on the principle that, in keeping with the
will of God, the nations form together a community with a
common aim and common duties. Even when the proclama-
tion of this principle gave rise to violent reactions, the Church
denied her assent to the erroneous concept of an absolutely
autonomous sovereignty divested of all social obligations.

"The Catholic Christian, persuaded that every man is his
neighbor and that every nation is a member, with equal rights,
of the family of nations, cooperates wholeheartedly in those
generous efforts whose beginnings might be meager and which
frequently encounter strong opposition and obstacles, but
which aim at saving individual states from the narrowness of a
self-centered mentality."

Everyone wants peace. But far too few Catholics in America
are willing to accept the internationalism which is a precondition, a prerequisite, indeed, the very instrument for achieving
peace. In many circles internationalism is a dirty word. But as
mature Christians we must want to conform our will and
thinking to the Church's and not try to conform the Church's
to our own often narrow and limited views. Before we reject
papal thinking we at least ought to make an effort to understand what it is.

Essentially, what papal thought seeks on the international
plane is the same as it desires on the national level in the
struggle to build a Christian social order: a reform of morals
and social (in this case, international) institutions. This
is the only possible solution for the problem of achieving and
maintaining a world peace. The popes are not starry-eyed
idealists by any means. What they are saying, however, is that
if real peace is to be achieved only a radical (i.e., root) solution

is the answer. Any attempts to reach an uneasy compromise will not bring lasting peace.

The popes insist that no individual nation should place its own interests before the common good of all nations. We must seek not America First but International Peace and World Order First. To some this will immediately sound un-American and rather foolish, but actually, of course, it is not. Ultimately, America must fit into a world order based on justice and charity if it is adequately to realize its best as a great nation and an international leader. And it is possible to do this, it should be noted, without the loss of our internal sovereignty.

As realists, experienced in diplomacy and world affairs, the popes comprehend that centuries of bad international habits cannot be overcome all at once; they have to be replaced by good habits and this process takes a long time. Peace doesn't just happen; it needs organized planning, plus much prayer and good will on all sides. War is not a moral problem alone; it also has its political, economic, psychological, military, and diplomatic aspects. But urging us on in the face of these complexities are the words of Christ: "Blessed are the peacemakers." (Though He is not saying "peace at any price.")

Like it or not, we are doubly committed to at least an awareness of international life. First, the other nations of the world society, from the most ancient to the most newly developed on the verge of applying for UN membership, will not let us forget that we live in a world that daily affects us; we simply cannot withdraw or escape from it even if we tried mightily to do so. And, second, as Catholics we must make our own the Christian internationalism so well described by Pius XII in his address to Pax Romana on April 27, 1957:

"The Christian therefore cannot remain indifferent to the evolution of the world. If he sees now in rough outline a development, under the pressure of events, of a constantly narrowing community, he knows that this unification, willed by the Creator, ought to culminate in a union of minds and hearts which is held together by a common faith and a common love.

Not only can he, but he must, work for the achievement of this community still in the process of formation. The example and plan of the Divine Master are, for him, a beacon and an incomparable source of strength. All men are his brothers, not only in virtue of their common origin and their participation in the same nature but also, in a more pressing way, in virtue of their common calling to the supernatural life."

Foolish? Too idealistic? If so, then Christ Himself is foolish and idealistic, for this is His Vicar speaking. And this is not a single isolated passage taken out of context. It is, rather, but a sample of his consistent and frequent preaching on the world community.

What is this peace, which Pius spent himself preaching? He answered this question in a 1940 address to Roman prelates in which he said that peace has a threefold aspect: First, individual peace of heart, which is a peace coming from order in the individual; in other words, the peace of Christ in a man's heart. Second, there is internal peace or peace in a particular state or nation, which will come from the establishment of order in each state, from peace between capital and labor, among the various elements of the social order. And, finally, there is external peace, or peace among nations. It should be noted that it is justice which removes the obstacles among men and as a result draws them more closely to solidarity; it is charity which binds men together.

To achieve this threefold peace, Pope Pius outlined, particularly in his Christmas Messages of the early years of World War II, a detailed plan based on the need for a twofold reconstruction of society: (1) Moral and (2) Institutional (especially political and economic institutions).

Here are some of the major points made by Pope Pius XII about the construction of a peaceful world:*

* For more detailed interpretations and commentaries we must turn to books such as Msgr. Harry Koenig's *Principles for Peace* and Guido Gonella's *The Papacy and World Peace*. The work of important commentators appears over the years in various issues of *Catholic Mind* and the Catholic Association for International Peace has produced some invaluable material. There is no substitute, of course, for the actual documents themselves; most of them have

1. *Reform of International Morality.* In his 1939 and 1940 Christmas Messages, Pius outlines what he considers the indispensable premises for a new world order:

First, the defeat of hatred, which is a barrier among nations. This will mean an end to those "systems and actions which breed this hatred"—especially propaganda. There must also be a defeat of mistrust, "which exerts a paralyzing pressure on international law and makes all honest understanding impossible."

Second, we must win a victory over utilitarianism, the disastrous theory which proclaims that utility is the basis and rule of right, that might makes right. This theory makes all international cooperation impossible.

Third, we must defeat the spirit of national egoism. This spirit, glorying in its own prowess, ends by violating not only the honor and sovereignty of states but also the rightful, proper, and disciplined liberty of citizens.

Fourth, there must be a return to a universal norm of morality.

Fifth, there must be a penetration of peoples and their governments by a spirit of responsibility based on justice and love.

2. *Reconstruction of International Order* (institutional reform). Some of the major reforms called for in this area are:

First, the recognition of the right to life and independence of all nations, large or small, strong or weak; one nation's will to live must never mean a death sentence for another nation. Men are not able to reach their ends in the natural order except through some joint action, which is the reason for forming states: for the common good. Liberty of citizenship is necessary for a man to reach his ends. In national life, order is realized by suppression of selfish individuals and this should also be the case among states.

Some rights which nations have are the right to be free from

appeared in the documentation section of *Catholic Mind* and are available also in other places and collections, such as *The Mind of Pius XII* by Robert C. Pollock and the more recent book by Harry W. Flannery, *Pattern for Peace.*

crushing, disproportionate armaments which lead to aggression; the rights of peoples, especially small ones, to have their own working men free from peonage to foreign capital; the right to be free from economic monopolies that concentrate the ownership and control of raw materials in the hands of a few nations and thus lead to jealousies and revolts; the right of each nation to have other nations together guarantee the inviolability of its frontiers; the right of each people to pursue its peaceful aims on land and sea without interference from commercial interests allied with military force.

Second, a liberal respect for the needs and just demands of nations and peoples as well as of ethnic minorities. This respect should extend to demands which, though they may not be strict rights, still deserve benevolent examination.

Third, the liberation of all nations from the heavy slavery of armaments and of the constant danger that material force, instead of serving to protect rights, might become the tyrannical violator of rights.

Pius XII recognized that disarmament is both a moral and a political problem. He was no utopian idealist; he insisted on adequate safeguards; but what he attempted to do was to set up an effective disarmament program to be worked for when feasible. Behind the idea of disarmament is the idea that men must give up force and violence and seek a peaceful solution to problems. It means more than merely taking arms from nations; there must be a moral disarmament as well. The recognition of disarmament as a moral problem is necessary even though it admittedly will be a long, slow process.

Pope Pius offered a realistic four-part program for disarmament: It must be *mutually accepted* by *all* nations. The program must be *organic*: It must start first with the strongest nations and with the most offensive weapons. It must be *progressive*: No nation will get rid of all its arms at once. All nations must be *faithful* to the agreement.

Fourth in the list of international institutional reforms is the need of economic reform. Among the chief causes of world tension, Pius said in 1948, is the economic inequity for some peoples suffering from a "comparative scantiness of national territory and the want of raw materials." This was an echo of his call in his 1940 Christmas Message for "the defeat of all that makes for the too great economic inequalities in the international sphere, those everlasting seeds of conflict. This will need gradual methods of improvement and accompanying guarantees so that a balance may be kept, if a settlement is to be achieved which will ensure to all peoples of every class a proper standard of living."

Our fifth point is one which has become needlessly controverted—the necessity of international juridical institutions. This is a complex problem in many respects, but one thing certainly seems to be clear without doubt and that is Pius XII's vigorous support of some form of international juridical institution to guarantee both the conditions of treaties and the preservation of the peace. It would be impossible for anyone to give even a cursory reading to the words of Pius XII without seeing this idea come through clearly time and time again.

And that this is more than merely a development in the thinking of Pius XII is made very clear by the universal acceptance of the idea by the bishops in each nation. At their semiannual meeting in the fall of 1960, for instance, the cardinals and archbishops of France wrote:

"Finally, the doctrine of the Church proclaims the necessity of an international organization of peoples to do away with the causes of conflicts, take jointly in hand the sufferings of humanity, the struggle against hunger, sickness, poverty in the world, ignorance. Together, all nations must work to save men, to assure the development in the economic, social, cultural fields of the young nations which have become independent, to defend and guarantee the moral values which are the foundations of true civilization and the authentic progress of humanity. Whatever may be the deficiencies inherent in any human institution, and however slow, patient, laborious its effort may be, an international organization of the nations is today more than ever indispensable to the establishment of world peace.

"Christians can and must participate in this great effort of international life, either on the level of the missionary apostolate or on the level of collaboration with the international organizations, or else on the level of mutual technical and professional aid."

In no one place did Pius XII spell out completely a detailed blueprint of what the international juridical organization he supported should look like. This, of course, is completely in accord with the usual papal approach of laying down general principles to be applied in the various nations according to local needs and circumstances. It can be seen, however, from a study of Pius XII's many pronouncements on the subject that he had some specific ideas. Perhaps in no one place did he outline them more completely than in his often quoted address of 1951 to the Fourth Congress of the World Movement for World Federal Government on "World Federalism."

"The Church desires peace," he said, "and therefore applies herself to the promotion of everything which, within the framework of the divine order, both natural and supernatural, contributes to the assurance of peace. Your movement dedicates itself to realizing an effective political organization of the world. Nothing is more in conformity with the traditional doctrine of the Church, nor better adapted to her teaching concerning legitimate or illegitimate war, especially in the present circumstances.

"It is necessary therefore to arrive at an organization of this kind, if for no other reason than to put a stop to the armament race in which, for decades past, the peoples have been ruining themselves and draining their resources to no effect."

Warning against too limited a view of the structure and function of an effective international organization, he added that "it is impossible to solve the problem of a world political organization without being willing to leave the beaten path from time to time, without appealing to the witness of history, to a sane social philosophy, and even to a certain divining of the creative imagination."

The thinking of Pius XII has been extended by Pope John in a variety of ways. His commendation of the International Labor Organization and the Food and Agriculture Organization of the United Nations in *Mater et Magistra*, plus his description of the Christian responsibility for aid to underdeveloped nations in the same document, is an accurate capsule of the trend of his international thought.

I have, till now, avoided mention of the United Nations, for it seems to me that the UN makes sense only within the complete context of Catholic thinking on international life. It is clear that the popes accepted the UN, realistically recognizing that it wasn't perfect and still needs constant improvement. But there is no evidence to indicate they were or are against it in principle or general practice. For those who feel the UN needs a defense, I refer them to Bishop James H. Griffiths, auxiliary bishop of New York and the American Hierarchy's representative at the UN. He gave a brilliant apologia for the United Nations in his address on "Our International Responsibility" to the annual meeting of the Catholic Association for International Peace in 1959.

But American Catholics still do not, as a group, know what they can do toward the promotion of peace and the understanding of international life. Yet, our responsibilities are heavy. In an address in 1952 on "Catholics and International Life," Pius XII noted that Catholics "are extraordinarily well equipped to collaborate in the creation of a climate without which a common action on the international plane can have neither substance nor prosperous growth." He added, "By the same token, of course, Catholics are saddled with a great responsibility. They above all, that is to say, must realize that they are called upon to overcome every vestige of nationalistic narrowness, and to seek a genuine fraternal encounter of nation with nation."

What can we American Catholic laymen do?

First, we must begin to understand what the Church's teachings on peace and international life are all about. We must study what the popes and the bishops have said. We must develop a basic understanding of the Church's teachings on this matter.

Second, we must make every effort to promote the understanding and consequences of these teachings among both Catholics and non-Catholics. So much depends on a widespread understanding of how we are to proceed in the cause of peace. But there will never be any chance of a concerted effort on the part of the people of America—Catholic and non-Catholic alike—unless they have a coherent set of principles to guide and enlighten them. Without a set of goals our efforts become fragmented and indecisive. We must use every effort to spread an understanding of Christian thought on internationalism and peace.

Third, we must become personally involved in the struggle for peace and international understanding, if only in a small, minor way. If the fight for peace is to become meaningful for us, I believe it essential that we participate actively in it in some way. One of the most simple acts we might perform is to invite a student from another land into our home for a visit or a holiday. This can be done easily through the foreign students' adviser of your local university. And many groups, such as the Christian Family Movement, lay mission groups, and others in many dioceses, have set up a regular service telling families how to invite students and how to entertain them. Or, you might assist the program of the National Catholic Welfare Conference to bring over high school students from other lands for a year by taking such a student into your home.

There are many small and meaningful actions which might be taken: corresponding with someone in another land, sending American books and magazines where they will do the most good abroad, sponsoring lectures on the Church and peace in your parish or diocese, joining a group such as the Catholic Association for International Peace—the list is limited only by the imagination of the individual.

Finally, of course, the easiest action we can take for peace is to heed the words of Mary at Fatima that, if we pray and do penance, in the end her Immaculate Heart will triumph and God would convert Russia and "an era of peace will be granted to mankind."

But perhaps the greatest lesson we need to learn is that international affairs and peace are no longer—if they ever were—solely the affair of diplomats. Foreign affairs are as close as the foreign student at your local educational institution. We can no longer ignore the world beyond our family circle.

"Christians cannot remain alien or indifferent to the present state of international affairs," the French cardinals and archbishops said in 1960. "They must be present in it by prayer, by knowledge of the doctrine of the Church in this domain, and by action."

CHAPTER 20

The Layman's Future

What will be the future of the American Catholic layman? Where is he going—and why? To rise above idle speculation, such questions must be considered in terms of avoiding past errors or helping us to prepare to meet new situations. With this purpose in mind, it might be instructive to examine some of the possible answers for the questions we have just raised.

One thing, I believe, is certain and it is that there is a new kind of layman abroad today who (often without realizing it) is going to see that things are different in the future. Within the Church he has been increasingly indoctrinated and educated in the meaning of what a layman really is and of his dignity, value, and importance. Already increasing numbers of laymen are beginning to view themselves differently; they are beginning to understand their responsibilities and duties—and, consequently, their rights. And outside the Church the American Catholic layman has achieved a new kind of social acceptance and status symbolized by the election of President Kennedy.

Thus, new things are beginning to happen to the layman, both as a Catholic and as a citizen. He is beginning to develop a new feeling of security, acceptance, and freedom, which is certainly going to be reflected in his future actions.

It is inevitable that tensions will arise and occasionally there may even be open conflicts of one kind or another in various parts of the Church as laymen try to feel their way in their new position in the Church and in American society. Some of these conflicts may be caused by members of the clergy who will, understandably enough, on occasion have some difficulty in adjusting habits and prerogatives of years' standing to new situations. Other difficulties are certain to arise as some lay-men, going through a stage of adolescent Christianity on the way to maturity, sometimes act like a bull in the china shop.

Father Congar has made it clear in his *Laity, Church and World* just how valuable all this possible difficulty and tension is. It is the good health of Holy Mother Church herself, he notes, that demands the layman to be active. It is sometimes more difficult to keep healthy children in hand, but then the layman too ill-instructed and indifferent to the Church to cause any difficulty is also too spiritless to do anything *for* the Church either.

The tensions and difficulties, it might be pointed out, are certain to arise on both sides of the fence. Some lay people are going to be discomfited by increasing appeals for them to accept a responsible role in the Church and to fulfill some minor chores. Already I have seen some instances of older, die-hard members of the laity shopping around for a parish church where they are *not* required to sing or participate actively in a dialogue Mass. Shades of the old days when the "shopping" was done to discover a church where the layman was *allowed* a modicum of participation!

How well we can learn from the past is well demonstrated by the relations between that fiery Catholic publicist and controversialist Orestes A. Brownson and Archbishop John Hughes of New York in 1860. Some of the exchanges as described by Fr. Thomas T. McAvoy in his article which appeared in the January, 1962, *Review of Politics* between this great layman and this outstanding churchman sound as if they might have taken place a hundred years later.

What were they discussing? Some of the same things clergy and laity are still discussing today: the role of the layman, the autonomy of the layman in the temporal order, the quality of Catholic education, freedom of speech within the Church. Some of Brownson's statements in his *Brownson's Quarterly Review* have—save for some of their direct forcefulness—a contemporary ring about them. For instance, in an essay on "Rights of the Temporal," in October, 1860, he wrote:

"There are persons, very excellent persons too, placed in positions of trust and influence, who think a Catholic publicist should resolutely defend everything Catholic, and especially everything said, done or approved by spiritual persons, direct all his attacks against outside barbarians, and studiously avoid agitating any question on which Catholics differ among themselves, or which may lead to discussions offensive or disagreeable to any portion of the Catholic community. . . .

"The evils which from time to time befall the Church, and often so great and deplorable, are in most cases, if not in all, far more attributable to the faults, errors, and blunders of Catholics themselves, than to the craftiness or wickedness of non-Catholics. . . ."

Speaking further of the autonomy of the laity in the temporal order, he added, rather pungently:

"In our age, when education and intelligence are not confined to the clergy, and are often possessed in as eminent degree by the laity as by them, when the most notable defences of Catholic history have been made by laymen, sometimes even by non-Catholics, and when the controversy between us and our enemies is removed from the sphere of theology, and made in the main a lay question, to be decided by the reason common to all men, rather than by authority, the fullest liberty must be given to laymen, compatible with the supremacy of the spiritual order and the discipline of the Church."

Some of my clerical (and lay!) friends become uneasy at such frank and direct writing. They are afraid of "trouble," "unnecessary conflict," "a split between the clergy and the laity." "Trouble" came for Brownson and "conflicts" will come for the laymen in the future, but let me state categorically that I believe the laymen who speak and write frankly and directly will never split from the clergy or the Church. Indeed, it is because of their great love of the Church and dedication to her and her best interests as they see them that they are impelled to write and speak in the hope they may improve her human aspects. I have been privileged because of my occupation as a journalist to be acquainted with some of the most outstanding and frank and controversial Catholic laymen of the 1940s, '50s and to the present. Never have I found one who was not thoroughly loyal to Christ and His Church *and* obedient to the will of his religious superiors.

When disagreements arose as a result of Brownson's clear-cut statements, some of the complaints against him—anonymous and otherwise—crossed the ocean to Rome. As a result, he wrote a letter, now in the Propaganda Archives in the Eternal City, which explained his position and his respect for legitimate authority, which I feel certain would be endorsed in principle by every leading layman today. Brownson wrote, in one part of the letter:

"Though the staunch advocate of all legitimate authority, however constituted, I am an American citizen and, for my own country, a Republican accustomed from my youth up to free thought and free speech; but the Prelates of the Church in the United States have only to signify to me under their own name the questions which they wish me not to discuss, or to give me frankly the directions they wish me to follow, to find me avoiding everything that could be offensive or disagreeable to them or inconsistent with the views of Catholic interests. I am and will be docile to authority, but I do not and cannot recognize the voice of authority in anonymous newspaper articles."

It is Brownson's rational loyalty and humility, reflected so well in increasing numbers of contemporary laymen, that provides the ray of hope for the future. For no matter what arguments may arise or differences of opinion erupt, I believe firmly that, without exception, lay leaders will show the docility and obedience asked of them by their religious superiors in the name of the Church, providing they are given such instructions frankly and directly, as Brownson notes in his characteristic independent American way.

Another study, published in *Ave Maria*, shows a further possible development in the future. In her study of the rise and fall of lay organizations from 1870 to 1920, Sister M. Adele Frances, O.S.F., has uncovered much valuable informa-

tion on the organized beginnings of the lay apostolate in the
United States, which is virtually unknown by most laymen.
Many of the lay groups of that period were ethnic or cultural
and most of them were defensive, that is, they existed to
protect the rights and interests of Catholics in such matters
as education, legal rights, and immigration.

The groups did well and prospered in their defensive role,
but ultimately they began to dissipate in number and strength.
They were finally absorbed into the official National Catholic
Welfare Conference.

We face a somewhat similar problem today in reverse, particularly in regard to the federal aid-to-education dispute.
Because there is no official Catholic opinion on the matter
and the unrest on the part of many laymen about the stands
on this political matter taken by some *official* Catholic groups,
a significant new approach is developing. To circumvent
unduly mixing the religious and the temporal and to avoid
creating religious misunderstandings and tensions, many laymen are now turning to the idea of creating *civic* groups to
achieve the goals they wish to attain as citizens, but goals
which also have some religious overtones. In this way, they do
not involve the Church and they are free to exercise their
autonomy as citizens in the temporal order. I think we can
look for increasing use of this approach in the future on the
part of laymen.

It seems quite likely that many varied new forms and outlets
for the lay apostolate will be experimented with in the future.
During the early days of this century the layman was active
in the Church through the kind of outlets that existed then;
at that time most of these were pious associations or the ethnic
or cultural groups we mentioned above. Then, during the
1920s and the early '30s, the layman was restricted in variety
and the number of different organized outlets for his interests
within the Church. There simply did not exist large numbers
of varied lay apostolic groups.

The situation began to change in the later 1930s as Catholic
Americans began to react to the social calamity of the Great

Depression by establishing such things as Catholic Worker houses and Hospitality Houses. Interest in the race question led to Friendship Houses and Catholic Interracial Councils; and a concern with the social question led to many labor schools and other social phenomena. After the war, beginning in the late 1940s, there developed the marriage and family movements, the Young Christian Nurses, and today even the grade school apostolate groups. The layman has an increasing number of channels for his interests, an ever-growing number of means by which he may participate in the life of the Church. There are so many groups, suited to so many tastes and interests, that the individual layman has fewer and fewer excuses for not participating.

And I believe this will continue in the future as new forms of the apostolate develop to meet new needs, or at least newly discovered needs. Further, outside the immediate limits of the Church, in the temporal order, it seems quite probable that laymen will begin to institute new means to work toward the Christianization of society. Until the inevitable reaction sets in at some far-distant date, the future will increasingly become an age of the organized apostolate.

The big question mark on the horizon is whether we shall meet the monumental challenge of the social formation of the coming generations of laymen. Although we are certainly doing much better than in the past, there is not the slightest indication that the future will bring a crash program of indoctrination and instruction in the social teachings of the Church. And yet this is the crucial question in regard to the impact of the Church in the community through its members.

In the first place, it will become increasingly true that in numbers there will be more and more Catholics present in the community—but will they be present as motivated and instructed Catholics or as religious nonentities, just part of the masses, more poor lambs in a nation of sheep?

I am tremendously concerned that Catholics be present *as Catholics* for many practical reasons. For one thing, the well-instructed Catholic can be immensely effective in society if only because he has a set of goals and some understanding—through a grasp of Catholic social doctrine—of where he wants society to go and how to lead it. Although the principles themselves are mainly and most often based on natural law thinking rather than dogma or Revelation, his personal religious formation will give the Catholic the perseverance and love to be present in the most difficult areas and conditions—for the love of Christ—even though this may require severe personal sacrifices on the human level. The contribution and cooperation of all men of good will are ultimately going to be needed for the construction of a society impregnated with love and justice. But should we not expect a greater commitment and a more profound willingness to sacrifice on the part of the convinced Christian as compared to the good pagan?

I see no evidence that we shall "save" the present generation in terms of social orientation and formation. But my great hope is for the children of the future, the children of the relatively small group of self-sacrificing parents in the family movements. Quietly and with great perseverance they have been rearing their children—often greater in number than most families—with a social awareness and training in the social principles of the Church that exceeds anything we have seen before in this century. My hope is that within the next generation these children and then their children will burst forth upon the scene in a kind of geometrical progression to change the social face of the Church in this nation. They will demonstrate, I believe, that all the work, worry, and weariness that went into the care and feeding of the family movement and the children who grew up in its atmosphere was eminently worth-while.

As we look at the future with its occasional black cloud on the horizon, we must more than ever exercise the virtue of hope and pray earnestly that the Holy Spirit will move quietly and quickly among the members of the Mystical Body around the world, but particularly in our own nation, refreshing, inspiring, enlightening. To buoy us up, we have the words of Pope John in *Mater et Magistra*:

"Although it must be admitted that the times in which we

live are torn by increasingly serious errors, and are troubled by violent disturbances, yet, it happens that the Church's laborers in this age of ours have access to enormous fields of apostolic endeavor. This inspires us with uncommon hope."

BIBLIOGRAPHY OF BOOKS MENTIONED

The American Catholic Family, by John L. Thomas, S.J. (Engle-wood Cliffs, New Jersey; Prentice-Hall, 1956).

American Catholics: A Protestant-Jewish View, edited by Philip Scharper (New York; Sheed & Ward, 1959).

The Catholic Church, U.S.A., edited by Louis J. Putz, C.S.C. (Chicago; Fides, 1956).

Catholics on Campus, by William J. Whalen (Milwaukee; Bruce, 1961).

Catholic Viewpoint on Censorship, by Harold C. Gardiner, S.J. (Garden City, New York; Doubleday Image Books, 1961).

Christians in the World, by Jacques Leclercq (New York; Sheed & Ward, 1961).

The Dynamics of Liturgy, by H. A. Reinhold (New York; Macmillan, 1961).

For Men of Action, by Yves de Montcheuil (Chicago; Fides, 1951).

Free Speech in the Church, by Karl Rahner, S.J. (New York; Sheed & Ward, 1959).

Frontiers in American Democracy, by Eugene J. McCarthy (Cleveland; World, 1960).

The Imitation of Christ, edited with an Introduction, by Edward J. Klein (New York; Harper & Brothers, 1943, 2nd ed.).

The Intelligent Woman's Guide to Conservatism, by Russell Kirk (New York; Devin-Adair, 1957).

Laity, Church and World, by Yves Congar, O.P. (Baltimore; Helicon, 1961).

The Layman's Call, by William R. O'Connor (New York; Kenedy, 1942).

Lay People in the Church, by Yves Congar, O.P., trans. by Donald Attwater (Westminster, Maryland; Newman Press, 1957).

The Mind of Pius XII, edited by Robert C. Pollock (New York; Crown, 1955).

The Papacy and World Peace, by Guido Gonella (Westminster, Maryland; Newman, 1950).

Pattern for Peace by Harry W. Flannery (Westminster, Maryland; Newman, 1961).

Priests Among Men, from *The Church Today: The Collected Writings of Emmanuel Cardinal Suhard* (Chicago; Fides, 1953).

Principles for Peace, by Harry C. Koenig (Milwaukee; Bruce, 1943).

Protestant Hopes and the Catholic Responsibility, by George Tavard (Chicago; Fides, 1960).

The Role of the Laity in the Church, by Gerard Philips (Chicago; Fides, 1956).

A *Saint in the Slave Trade*, by Arnold Lunn (New York, Sheed & Ward, 1935).

The Third Revolution, by Karl Stern (Garden City, New York; Doubleday Image Books, 1961).

Virgil Michel and the Liturgical Movement, by Paul B. Marx, O.S.B. (Collegeville, Minnesota; Liturgical Press, 1957).